Disclaimer

The publisher of this book is by no way associated with the National Institute of Standards and Technology (NIST). The NIST did not publish this book. It was published by 50 page publications under the public domain license.

50 Page Publications.

Book Title: A Numerical Model for Combustion of Bubbling Thermoplastic Materials in Microgravity

Book Author: Kathryn M. Butler;

Book Abstract: A numerical model is demonstrated for the pyrolysis of a spherical thermoplastic sample in microgravity including effects of bubbles. The model combines nucleation, growth, and migration of individual bubbles in 3-D space with a finite element model that solves the 1-D radial equation for the temperature field. Energy calculations include surface losses due to radiation and convection, conductive heat transfer through the mixture of gaseous and condensed phase material, and the chemistry of gasification. Gases released by bursting bubbles determine the mass loss rate from the sample.

Citation: NIST Interagency/Internal Report (NISTIR) - 6894

Keyword: bubbles;combustion;finite element model;microgravity;numerical model;pyrolysis;thermoplastic materials

NISTIR 6894

A Numerical Model for Combustion of Bubbling Thermoplastic Materials in Microgravity

Kathryn M. Butler

National Institute of Standards and Technology
Technology Administration, U.S. Department of Commerce

A Numerical Model for Combustion of Bubbling Thermoplastic Materials in Microgravity

Kathryn M. Butler
Fire Research Division
Building and Fire Research Laboratory
National Institute of Standards and Technology
Gaithersburg, MD 20899-8665

August 2002

U.S. DEPARTMENT OF COMMERCE
Donald L. Evans, Secretary
TECHNOLOGY ADMINISTRATION
Phillip J. Bond, Under Secretary of Commerce for Technology
NATIONAL INSTITUTE OF STANDARDS AND TECHNOLOGY
Arden L. Bement, Jr., Director

Contents

Abstract

A numerical model is demonstrated for the pyrolysis of a spherical thermoplastic sample in microgravity including effects of bubbles. The model combines nucleation, growth, and migration of individual bubbles in three-dimensional space with a finite element model that solves the one-dimensional radial equation for the temperature field. Energy calculations include surface losses due to radiation and convection, conductive heat transfer through the mixture of gaseous and condensed phase material, and the chemistry of gasification. Gases released by bursting bubbles determine the mass loss rate from the sample.

Results demonstrate the thermally insulating properties of bubbles as they transport gases to the surface of a heated polymeric sample. The mass loss rate is particularly sensitive to the bursting process, since slow drainage from the thin film defining the bubble at the surface maintains gases of low thermal conductivity as a thermal barrier to slow the transport of heat. The behaviors of pyrolyzing PMMA and PP spheres are investigated.

Acknowledgments

Helpful conversations with Dr. Sandra Olson of NASA, Dr. Indrek Wichman of Michigan State University, and Drs. Jiann Yang, Anthony Hamins, Takashi Kashiwagi, and Nicos Martys of NIST are gratefully acknowledged. This research was funded by the NASA Glenn Research Center under NASA Interagency Agreement C-32033-E.

1 Introduction

Polymeric materials are easily molded into complex shapes, are relatively light-weight, and may be tailored to a specific task by modification of properties through chemical composition and the use of additives. These highly attractive properties have made polymers as ubiquitous in space vehicles as they are in houses, office buildings, and transportation vehicles. The flammability of these materials poses a challenge for the fire safety of personnel and spacecraft. To make wise choices about spacecraft design and their fire suppression systems, we must improve our understanding of how polymeric materials burn in a microgravity environment.

Combustion behavior in microgravity differs from that in normal-gravity environments. The primary difference is in the elimination of buoyancy-driven flow, which considerably reduces the convection of heat and combustion products away from the flame and of oxygen into the flame. In early microgravity experiments on paraffin, neoprene, foam rubber, and other combusting solids in a quiescent environment [1], the flames did not reach a steady-state but gradually darkened and shrank in size. Some samples self-extinguished. These experiments supported the conclusion that combustion is less hazardous at low gravity. Testing of fire hazards in normal gravity was therefore assumed to adequately assess the behavior of burning materials in low gravity.

The behavior of polymeric materials during pyrolysis and combustion is highly complex. As the temperature rises, the molecules in a thermoplastic solid become increasingly mobile, giving the material the viscous properties of a fluid. For some polymers, a phase change from solid to liquid takes place; for others, the viscosity changes more slowly with temperature. Chemical bond breaking reduces the average molecular weight of the polymer, further reducing the viscosity. The breaking of bonds eventually results in polymer fragments that are small enough to constitute gas molecules. Conduction of heat from the surface often results in gasification deep within the polymeric melt, causing formation of internal bubbles, swelling of the outer surface, and sputtering of gases and small droplets as the bubbles burst [3]. The bubbles act as a mechanism for the mass transport of volatile gases. They also affect the transport of heat by decreasing the local thermal conductivity, causing convection of the surrounding fluid, and changing the internal absorption of radiation. As they burst, the bubbles may expose a larger region near the surface to chemical attack from the surrounding gases (such as oxygen). This effect is due to entrainment and, for highly viscous melts, to the distortion of the surface geometry.

The bursting of bubbles results in a fire hazard unique to microgravity. In combustion experiments on Velcro fasteners made of nylon [4], the ignition of flammable gases from a bursting bubble resulted in flamelets spurting from the flame zone. Occasionally, burning liquid droplets were expelled from the sample with velocities higher than 30 cm/s. These droplets burned robustly until all fuel was consumed, demonstrating a potential to contribute to the spread of fire by serving as hot ignition sources. Bursting fuel vapor bubbles were also observed in the WIF experiment [5], which studied the burning behavior of polyethylene insulation covering a nichrome wire in both quiescent and flowing air. Bubble bursting was inferred by pulsations of the flame and ejection of small particles of molten polyethylene.

The purpose of the numerical model described in this report is to improve our understanding of the development of bubbles in a burning thermoplastic object and their effects on heat and mass transport under microgravity conditions. The model was designed to help understand experimental data from combusting spheres of polypropylene (PP) and polymethylmethacrylate (PMMA) collected under a NASA grant headed by Dr. Jiann Yang [6],[7].

The bubble model combines a one-dimensional (radial) finite element model of a sphere with the behavior of individual bubbles located in three-dimensional space. The thermoplastic sphere is initialized as a volume of highly viscous material divided into a specified number of elements of equal volume in the shape of concentric spherical shells. Each element is a "material volume" of polymeric material; the element travels with the same chunk of polymer throughout the calculation, although the amount of polymer decreases with time as it gasifies.

At the beginning of the calculation, a bubble nucleation site is placed at a random location within each element. Each bubble is initialized with zero volume. A heat flux is applied to the outer surface of the thermoplastic sphere, and the energy equation is solved to determine the temperature field at the next timestep. Radiative and convective losses at the surface are included. As the sphere heats, the polymer contained in each element gasifies according to a first order Arrhenius expression. This gas collects in the bubble associated with the element, which grows and migrates toward the surface of the sphere due to the viscosity and surface tension gradients caused by the temperature gradient within the element. If the midpoint of the bubble has exceeded a specified distance from the surface of the sphere and satisfied a delay time representing the time required to drain the thin film between surface and bubble, the bubble is presumed to burst. The mass of its gaseous contents is then subtracted from the spherical sample.

At the end of the timestep, the size, location, and content (polymer and gas) of each element are recomputed and the material properties are determined by the properties of polymer and gas weighted by their respective volume fractions. The energy equation is solved again, and the process continues.

2   Background

There are a limited number of theoretical and numerical models of materials that bubble and foam when they are heated. Many of these models simplify by solving a one-dimensional heat transfer problem with an incident heat flux at one surface.

Wichman studied the effect of in-depth bubbles on the steady-state transport of volatile gases from a thermoplastic material subjected to a conductive incident heat flux theoretically [8]. Bubble nucleation, growth, and convection were incorporated into the bubble number distribution function. Writing the conservation equations for mass, momentum, species, and energy in terms of this distribution function enabled the determination of a steady-state regression rate.

Several one-dimensional models have been developed to model the foaming behavior of intumescent fire-resistant coatings. These coatings provide protection to an underlying surface through the production of bubbles in a charring thermoplastic medium. An endothermic gasification reaction generates bubbles in the molten thermoplastic, and the gas trapped in the final swollen char provides an insulating barrier to the transport of heat. The expansion and expansion rate due to bubble growth were shown to be of critical importance to the transport of heat by single-layer [9], [10] and two-layer models [11].

The development of two- and three-layer frontal models was based on the observation that intumescence takes place within a thin region, with solidification freezing the geometry in place once the front has passed. Anderson et al. [12] used an equivalent thermal resistance model to estimate the effective thermal conductivity of intumescent chars. In each of these models, swelling due to the formation of bubbles was provided as an input parameter rather than being determined from first principles. The goal of these models was to understand the heat transfer mechanisms protecting the underlying substrate from excessive temperature rises. The migration and bursting of bubbles at the surface was not addressed.

Bubble nucleation and growth in a melting solid have also been studied in the field of coal pyrolysis. When most coals are heated, they swell to a much larger volume until they reach a critical final swelling temperature. During the swelling, the coal behaves like a highly viscous liquid, and gas-producing chemical reactions generate bubbles. Attar modelled the mechanism of bubble nucleation theoretically [13]. Oh wrote a mathematical model to predict volatile yields, plasticity, and swelling during softening coal pyrolysis and compared the results with experiment [14], [15]. This model treated the coal particles as spherical and isothermal, with a spatially uniform bubble concentration. Gas diffusion, chemical reactions, coalescence, and bubble rupture upon contact with the particle surface were included. Because of the highly viscous nature of softening coal, the model neglected bubble movement.

A numerical model of high-energy, strained-molecule fuel droplets by Schiller et al. [16] considered the bubbles generated by the fuel vaporizing in depth. The model solved time-dependent equations in three-dimensions representing continuity, energy and species conservation, and radial bubble growth. Exothermic chemical reactions and local average mixture thermal conductivity and bubble densities were included. Bubbles burst, releasing fuel vapor and shrinking the droplet size, when the void fraction of the bubbles reached unity in the region close to the droplet surface. The intermittent bursting of bubbles caused the droplet size to alternately expand and contract with time. Migration of the bubbles in space was not considered in this model.

A three-dimensional, time-dependent numerical model of burning thermoplastic materials with in-depth bubble formation developed at NIST included the dynamics of bubble growth and migration, heat transfer through the material, and the chemistry of gasification [17]. However, this model was unsuccessful in incorporating thermal effects of the bubbles.

3 Microgravity Experiments on Polymer Spheres

A series of microgravity experiments to investigate combustion of supported thermoplastic spheres were performed aboard the NASA DC-9 and KC-135 Reduced Gravity Aircraft by a team led by Jiann Yang [6], [7]. Burning histories were recorded on videotape at 35 frames per second for polymethylmethacrylate (PMMA), polypropylene (PP), and polystyrene (PS) under various conditions of pressure and oxygen concentration. Events observed during combustion include bubbling, sputtering, soot shell formation and breakup, and ejection of material from the burning spheres. This author was privileged to observe some of these experiments in person.

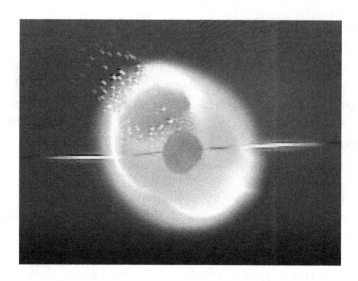

Figure 1: A PMMA sphere in the first few seconds after ignition, with a relatively undisturbed spherical flame front.

The behavior of a combusting polymer sphere proceeds as follows. The sphere is covered with a large number of bubbles almost immediately upon ignition. As the bubbles grow, the population appears to be monodisperse in size until bubble bursting is observed. For the first few seconds of burning, as shown in Figure 1, the flame front is relatively quiescent and nearly spherical except for a minor asymmetry caused by g-jitter in the aircraft. This is followed by the sudden onset of violent ejection events, which continue at an average frequency of 3 Hz for PMMA and 5 Hz for PP and PS until the fuel is gone [7].

Two distinct types of ejection events are observed [18]. In the first, observed during combustion of every polymer sample, the flame front shows a large disturbance whose length is on the order of the flame thickness. In the video, this flamelet appears suddenly from one video frame to the next, and decays over a few tenths of a second, as shown in Figure 2. The structures displayed in these two sequences are suggestive of vortex-flame front interactions such as those studied by Roberts and Driscoll [20] and Renard et al. [21].

In the second type of ejection event, a burning particle is emitted from the sphere. Unlike the previously-described gaseous events, this event does not significantly distort the flame front, and the burning droplet travels in a straight line away from the sphere, as shown in Figure 3. Unfortunately, the luminosity of the flame front surrounding the droplet prevents the measurement of its size. During the microgravity experiments, PP samples were observed to eject a considerable number of particles, while none were observed for PMMA.

The sequence of events for a bursting bubble has been photographed by Newitt et al. [22]. As the bubble reaches the surface from within the fluid, the outer surface forms a dome while the internal bubble pressure maintains a depression at the inner interface. Liquid drains from the dome until it breaks into a cloud of droplets on the order of ten microns in size. The bubble gases are released under pressure, likely generating vortices in the quiescent environment and transporting the tiny droplets. The depression left by the escaping gases collapses into a central jet, which may break up into one or more

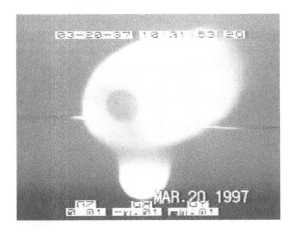

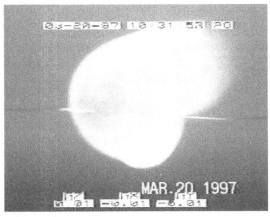

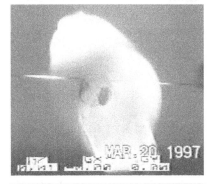

Figure 2: Images from combustion of thermoplastic spheres in microgravity. On the left is a sequence of frames showing a developing flamelet in side view. In the previous frame, the lower surface of the flamefront was undisturbed. On the right is a sequence showing a flamelet apparently emitted toward the camera.

5

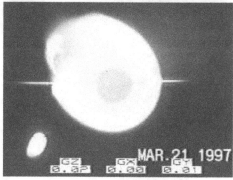

Figure 3: A particle emitted from a PP sphere. The particle is only visible for these two frames.

relatively large drops (≈ 0.1 mm to 1 mm in diameter) travelling at a speed which may initially exceed a thousand cm per second [23].

The gas expelled from the bursting bubble and the droplets produced by jet breakup provide good explanations for the two types of ejection events from combusting polymer spheres. Droplet size measurements by Tomaides and Whitby [23] suggest a wave-form disturbance in the bubble film during film rupture. The breakup of the resulting concentric toroids into nearly monodisperse droplets could account for the concentric rings that frequently appear in flamelet events such as that shown in the right-hand sequence of Figure 2. The breakup of the central jet into droplets is highly sensitive to the physical properties of the liquid. Since the viscosity of a molten polymer is dependent on molecular weight, it is not surprising that jet breakup occurs more readily for PP, which degrades by random scission, than for PMMA, which unzips to monomer during thermal degradation [24] and therefore remains a high-viscosity melt.

Measurements of thermoplastic sphere diameter with time showed that the average burning rates increase with initial sphere diameter and oxygen concentration. The burning rate of PP is slower than that of PMMA and PS. Due to swelling, the measured sphere diameter remains approximately steady for about half of the total burn duration, after which time the square of the diameter linearly decreases with time.

4 Theory

As shown in Figure 4, the computational problem to be solved is that of a spherical sample of thermoplastic material exposed to a heat flux uniformly over its surface. The amount of heat that actually enters the sample is reduced by reflective, convective, and radiative losses. At a given time the sample may contain numerous bubbles of a variety of sizes. Each bubble grows in time and migrates toward the surface, where it bursts and releases its gases. The presence of bubbles within the thermoplastic sample affects the transport of both heat and mass.

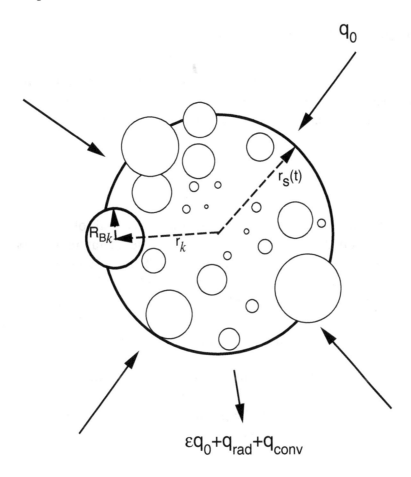

Figure 4: Bubbling thermoplastic sphere model.

Bubble development and behavior in a heated polymer are very complex. Since the glass temperature is often well below the temperature of gasification, bubbles appear due to either homogeneous nucleation or, in the presence of impurities, heterogeneous nucleation. As a bubble moves through the melt due to Marangoni (surface tension gradient) forces and forces due to gradients in viscosity resulting from the temperature gradient, it continues to grow by diffusion of the gases generated nearby. The bubble slows as it approaches the sample surface, where the thin film between the bubble and the gaseous environment outside the sample drains until the bubble bursts and delivers its gases to the surroundings. The release of condensed phase droplets that may accompany the bursting process [22], [23] is not considered in this model.

In order to include the details of bubble phenomena in a model whose main interest is in the combustion behavior of the thermoplastic sample as a whole, the approach to this problem separates phenomena into two systems that undergo separate analysis but strongly interact. The bubble submodel follows the growth, migration, and eventual bursting of each individual bubble according to the local conditions at the bubble location. The mixture submodel studies the evolution of the heated thermoplastic sample as a whole, including the temperature field and mass loss rate, by treating the bubble-containing polymer as a mixture whose bulk material properties are an appropriately weighted average of gas and melt properties, with spatial dependence on radius alone.

4.1 One-Fluid Mixture Submodel

Since the basic problem for the gas/melt mixture is that of a sphere surrounded by a uniform heat flux, the problem is spherically symmetric. The equations of mass, velocity, and energy, along with their initial conditions and boundary conditions, are therefore functions of radius and time only.

4.1.1 Mass Balance

The two components in this problem are polymer and gas, both of which are treated as fluids. The transformation of the polymer from a solid to a melt as the temperature rises above the glass temperature is handled through changes in the polymer viscosity. The densities of polymer and gas are defined locally as $\rho_p = M_p/V_p$ and $\rho_g = M_g/V_g$ respectively, where M_p is the mass of a small volume V_p of polymer and M_g is the mass of a small volume V_g of gas. The local volume fractions of polymer and gas are $\phi_p = V_p/V$ and $\phi_g = V_g/V$, where $V = V_p + V_g$ is the total volume. The sum of local volume fractions is equal to one, and the initial conditions are $\phi_p = 1$ and $\phi_g = 0$.

Mass is exchanged between the two components of polymer and gas as the thermoplastic sample is heated. Because conservation of mass requires that the total mass remain constant, whatever is lost from the polymer must be gained by the gas and vice versa. For many polymers, including those considered in this report, the rate of mass loss $\dot{m}$ as a function of temperature T is adequately described by a first order Arrhenius expression,

$$\dot{m} = \rho_p \phi_p B \exp(-E/RT) \quad , \tag{1}$$

where B and E are the pre-exponential constant and activation energy respectively for the gasification reaction and R is the universal gas constant [25]. Therefore, assuming that all variables and material properties depend on radius alone and act in the radial direction only, the mass balance equations for the polymer and gas components in a spherical geometry are

$$\frac{\partial \rho_p \phi_p}{\partial t} + \frac{1}{r^2} \frac{\partial}{\partial r} \left(\rho_p \phi_p r^2 W_p \right) = -\rho_p \phi_p B \exp(-E/RT) \tag{2}$$

8

$$\frac{\partial \rho_g \phi_g}{\partial t} + \frac{1}{r^2} \frac{\partial}{\partial r} \left(\rho_g \phi_g r^2 W_g \right) = \rho_p \phi_p B \exp(-E/RT) \quad , \tag{3}$$

where W_p is the radial velocity of the polymer and W_g is the radial velocity of the gas.

The sum of these two equations demonstrates the conservation of total mass,

$$\frac{\partial \rho^*}{\partial t} + \frac{1}{r^2} \frac{\partial}{\partial r} \left(\rho^* r^2 W^* \right) = 0 \quad , \tag{4}$$

where the total mass density is

$$\rho^* = \rho_p \phi_p + \rho_g \phi_g \tag{5}$$

and the barycentric velocity is

$$W^* = \frac{\rho_p \phi_p W_p + \rho_g \phi_g W_g}{\rho^*} \quad . \tag{6}$$

4.1.2 Momentum Equations

As the polymer gasifies, the gases collect in bubbles, which move through the melt due to a Marangoni (surface tension gradient) force and to a viscosity gradient force, both of which result from gradients in the temperature of the polymer melt. Both forces drive a bubble in the direction from lower to higher temperatures. Since the temperature is highest toward the surface of the sphere, the radial velocity of the gaseous component is expected to be positive. The velocity of the polymer melt at a given radial location may be positive, reflecting the swelling caused by bubble growth within the sphere, or negative as the melt fills in regions that have lost polymer to gasification. Gas and polymer velocities are needed to determine the barycentric velocity for use in the energy equation.

Standard continuum momentum equations, such as the Navier-Stokes equation for fluids or Darcy's law for porous media, are not used to determine the separate velocities for polymer and gas components. These velocities are determined instead by gasification chemistry and bubble dynamics. A description of the derivation of radial bulk mixture velocities from the bubble submodel is given in section 5.9.

4.1.3 Energy Equation

For a one-fluid description of a multi-component fluid mixture, the components are assumed to be in thermal equilibrium, so that $T_p = T_g = T$. This is a reasonable assumption for the problem at hand since the ratio of gas and polymer thermal capacities, $\rho_p (c_p)_p / \rho_g (c_p)_g$ is large. Other simplifying assumptions are:

- No internal radiation; all heat losses due to radiation occur at the surface

- The variation of chemical potential with temperature can be ignored

- Energy dissipation due to friction is neglected

- Polymer and gas are incompressible fluids; expansivity $\beta = 0$ and effects of pressure are not included.

Appendix A demonstrates how an equation for temperature can be derived directly from the internal energy equation using the principles of irreversible thermodynamics. Using the above assumptions, the energy equation for this spherically symmetric geometry is

$$(\rho c_p)^* \left[\frac{\partial T}{\partial t} + W^* \frac{\partial T}{\partial r} \right] = \frac{1}{r^2} \frac{\partial}{\partial r} \left(r^2 k^* \frac{\partial T}{\partial r} \right) - H_v \dot{m} \qquad (7)$$

where k^* is the effective thermal conductivity, H_v is the (positive) heat of vaporization and mass loss rate $\dot{m}$ is given by the Arrhenius expression in equation (1).

The solution must satisfy the appropriate initial and boundary conditions. Initially, the temperature throughout the thermoplastic sample is the ambient temperature:

$$T(r, 0) = T_0 \qquad . \qquad (8)$$

At the surface of the sphere, the heat flux into the sample is given by the incident heat flux minus losses due to reflectivity, convection, and radiation:

$$\text{at } r = r_S(t), \qquad -k^* \frac{\partial T}{\partial r} = \epsilon q_0 + \epsilon \sigma_{SB} \left(T^4 - T_0^4 \right) + h_c (T - T_0) \qquad , \qquad (9)$$

where q_0 is the incident heat flux, ϵ is the surface emissivity, σ_{SB} is the Stefan-Boltzman constant, and h_c is the convective coefficient. The surface emissivity is equal to one minus the surface reflectivity, and is the fraction of the incident radiation that enters the bulk of the sample. At the center of the sphere, the temperature must be physically attainable; the values must be finite and the field must be smooth. Therefore,

$$\text{at } r = 0, \quad \frac{\partial T}{\partial r} = 0 \qquad (10)$$

4.1.4 Effective Thermal Conductivity

The effective thermal conductivity of a material consisting of multiple components depends on the geometrical configuration of the components as well as on the thermal conductivity of each. In the literature on thermal decomposition of materials, many authors [26], [27], [29] choose to represent thermal conductivity by a volume-weighted average, or parallel arrangement, of the properties of the N_c components,

$$k^* = \sum_j^{N_c} \phi_j k^*_j \quad . \tag{11}$$

This expression describes an upper limit of k^* in which the components connect the heat source directly through the material. This is a good description in cases in which the component with highest conductivity is well-connected throughout. A series description of effective thermal conductivity,

$$\frac{1}{k^*} = \sum_j^{N_c} \frac{\phi_j}{k^*_j} \quad , \tag{12}$$

has been used to model intumescent coatings as a thermal resistance network [12]. In this limit, the components are treated as layers running parallel to the surface, providing an insulating effect that is dominated by the component with lowest conductivity.

In the case considered here, low thermal conductivity bubbles are completely surrounded by the polymer melt, which has much higher thermal conductivity. The parallel arrangement could therefore be argued to be a reasonable approximation. However, observations of the burning spheres show that a bubbly layer, with bubbles tightly packed, forms on the sample surface within the first second or two following ignition. The resulting thin polymer films will not conduct heat as well as wide regions of melt. For reasonable treatment of both conditions, the geometric mean approximation [30]

$$k^* = (k_p)^{\phi_p} (k_g)^{\phi_g} \quad . \tag{13}$$

is chosen in this work to estimate an effective thermal conductivity for each element. This combination of gas and polymer thermal conductivities predicts a value between those given by the parallel and series limits.

4.2   Bubble Submodel

Experimental and theoretical studies of bubble nucleation, growth, and migration in the polymer literature have related primarily to the production of foams and to the devolatilization step in polymer processing. Polymer foams are produced through expansion of a supersaturated solution of a blowing agent added to a polymer melt. During devolatilization, volatile components such as unreacted monomers, solvents, and precipitators (e.g. water) are removed after polymerization by reducing the ambient pressure below the equilibrium partial pressure of the volatile gases at an elevated temperature. In both cases an isothermal situation may be assumed, since production of gases is primarily induced by a change in pressure.

To the knowledge of the author, the details of bubble generation in the complex and highly nonisothermal case of thermoplastic materials undergoing thermal degradation have not been investigated. In the absence of such studies, approaches suggested by the polymer foam and devolatilization literature are used to treat bubble behavior in this model.

4.2.1 Bubble Nucleation

Current understanding of the process of bubble nucleation in polymer foams [31], [32] suggests the following steps for a thermoplastic material undergoing pyrolysis:

- The energy added to the material during heating translates to molecular motion, so that the polymer is considered to be in a melted state.

- A thermal fluctuation causes fragmentation of polymer molecules in a local region. Volatile products of degradation form a cluster of gas molecules which constitutes the bubble "seed" or nucleus.

- If the cluster exceeds a critical size for which free energy of cluster formation is a maximum, it grows by kinetics as gas molecules collide with the cluster. The free energy may be thought of as an energy barrier that must be overcome in order for nucleation to occur.

- The growing cluster reaches the critical size for bubble formation, for which the bubble is in thermal, chemical, and mechanical equilibrium with the polymer. At this point the gas molecules are separated from the liquid molecules by an interface.

- Growth of the supercritical bubble proceeds by diffusion in addition to surface tension, inertial, and heat-transfer forces.

This process is known as homogeneous nucleation. The alternate process of heterogeneous nucleation requires the presence of physical impurities to provide the seeds of bubble formation. Although commercial polymers may contain such sites, heterogeneous nucleation is not necessary for significant bubbling to take place, as suggested by recent advances in nucleation theory and by experiments in which adding fine particles to a polymer melt has only minor effects on bubbling behavior [38].

The classical molecular theory of nucleation assumes that critical bubbles can be described in terms of bulk thermodynamic properties. The nucleation rate per unit volume J is related linearly to the number of molecules per unit volume of the metastable (liquid) phase M and a frequency factor B, and exponentially to the free energy change $\triangle F_{cr}$ required to form the critical bubble [33], [34]:

$$J = MB \exp\left(\frac{-\triangle F_{cr}}{k_B T}\right) \tag{14}$$

where k_B is Boltzmann's constant and T is temperature. The frequency factor describes the frequency with which the bubble seed comes into contact with gas molecules. For boiling of a single component liquid, the frequency factor is

$$B = (2\sigma/\pi m C)^{1/2} \tag{15}$$

where σ is the surface tension at the liquid-gas interface, m the mass of the gas molecule, and C a coefficient related to the ratio of liquid phase pressure P_L to vapor pressure P_V. For a mixture in which one component is volatile, assuming Henry's law relating pressure to concentration holds, B is estimated as [33]

$$B \approx D(C_V - C_L)(k_B T/\sigma)^{1/2} \tag{16}$$

where D is the diffusion coefficient for the volatile in the liquid and C_V and C_L are equilibrium concentrations at P_V and P_L respectively.

Direct application of the classical theory to bubble formation in polymer melts resulted in predictions of nucleation rate many orders of magnitude smaller than those observed in experiments [35]. Han and Han [34] modified the classical theory to include the presence of macromolecules and the degree of supersaturation in the free energy term, introduce empirical relations for the frequency factor and bubble growth, and account for the consumption of a finite quantity of gas:

$$J = B_1 \frac{D}{4\pi r_c^2} M \exp\left(\frac{-B_2}{T}\right) \exp\left(\frac{-\triangle F^*}{n k_B T}\right) \quad , \tag{17}$$

where B_1 and B_2 are empirically determined constants, n is the number of gas molecules in a critical bubble, $\triangle F^*$ is the modified change in free energy, and $D = D(T)$ is the diffusivity of the volatile molecule in the polymer solution [36]. This model predicts nucleation rates on the order of $J \approx 10^{13}$ to 10^{19} bubbles/cm^3-s at temperatures from 150 °C to 180 °C. Good agreement with experiment is not yet achieved by this model. Bubble population density from experiment was found to be roughly four orders of magnitude smaller than that determined by the modified theory, possibly attributable in part to bubble coalescence, which is not included in the theory.

As a final note, bubble nucleation is also affected by the presence of elastic stresses, which lower the free energy required for critical cluster formation. Since elastic stresses result from the deformation of macromolecules in the vicinity of an existing bubble, the formation of small satellite bubbles near a primary bubble, also referred to as secondary nucleation, may occur. This phenomenon is noted for elastomers by Gent and Tompkins [37] and studied in detail for viscoelastic fluids by Yarin et al. [38], who include molecular relaxation in their analysis. Secondary nucleation may provide an explanation for the "frosted" appearance of some bubbles formed within burning PMMA in experiments by Olson [39]. The model for bubbles used in this work does not include secondary nucleation, but its implications for bubble growth are discussed in the next subsection.

4.2.2 Bubble Growth

The rate of volatile gas generation due to polymer degradation at a given temperature can be described by the Arrhenius expression in equation (1). Given this chemical model, the quantity of gas produced in a given time increment and within a given radial shell can be treated as a known quantity. One question that arises is whether it is reasonable to distribute this gas immediately among nearby bubbles (i.e. assuming mass diffusion time rapid compared to the thermal time scale), or whether some amount must be partitioned off into a reservoir of individual molecules dispersed throughout the polymer melt.

For a bubble in a single component fluid, the growth process is controlled by a succession of forces. Initial growth from the critical size is dominated by surface tension forces and very slow. As inertial forces become dominant, growth is driven primarily by the difference between the vapor pressure within the bubble and the external pressure, and the growth rate is linear with time. Finally, evaporation caused by heat transfer from the surrounding liquid to the lower temperature of the bubble wall predominates, and the growth rate becomes proportional to $t^{1/2}$.

In a liquid-gas solution, the gas concentration is a critical variable, and diffusion is often the controlling factor. A simple diffusion-controlled bubble growth problem, neglecting surface tension and convective mass transport, was solved analytically by Epstein and Plesset [40], who found the growth rate of a spherical gas bubble in an oversaturated solution to be

$$\frac{dR}{dt} = DS \left(\frac{P_0}{P_V} - 1 \right) \left[\frac{1}{R} + \frac{1}{(\pi Dt)^{1/2}} \right] \quad , \tag{18}$$

where D is the coefficient of diffusivity and S the gas solubility. An approximate solution to this equation is [37]

$$R = 2 \left(\pi Dt \right)^{1/2} \gamma \left[\gamma + \left(1 + \gamma^2 \right)^{1/2} \right] \quad , \tag{19}$$

where $\gamma^2 = S[(P_0/P_V) - 1]/2\pi$. The rate of change of volume $(4\pi/3)R^2 dR/dt$ for a bubble under fixed conditions of D, S, and P_0/P_V is therefore approximately proportional to R.

A rigorous model of diffusion-induced growth in viscoelastic fluids including convection, diffusion, surface tension, and inertial effects for a variety of viscoelastic constitutive relations was performed by Venerus et al. [41]. This analysis showed that the bubble growth rate in a viscoelastic fluid is bounded below by growth in a Newtonian fluid and above by diffusion-controlled growth, and that the effects of nonlinear fluid rheology are minor relative to elasticity effects.

This and other literature on diffusion-induced growth could be used to develop a reasonable partitioning into bubbles and solution for gases generated by polymer degradation at high temperatures. Alternatively, a simpler assumption of instantaneous distribution to bubbles has a theoretical and experimental basis for melts with elastic properties.

Devolatilization experiments performed by Yarin et al. [38] on a variety of polymers with shear-thinning behavior showed a large number of "microblisters" a few tenths of micrometers in size located on the walls between large primary bubbles one or two magnitudes larger in size. This is a secondary nucleation phenomenon, in which fluid motions due to the growth of a primary bubble in a polymer melt cause deformation of nearby macromolecules and introduce elastic stresses. The accumulation of elastic energy associated with these stresses leads to rapid mechanical degradation of nearby macromolecules and lowers the free energy barrier for the formation of new bubble nuclei. These secondary nuclei grow due to diffusion or internal gas pressure and may coalesce with the primary bubble, considerably accelerating the effective growth of this bubble. Theoretical analysis confirms a high secondary bubble nucleation rate in the neighborhood of primary bubbles larger than a few micrometers. When stress relaxation in the polymer melt is included, the nucleation rate remains high as long as the growth rate of the primary bubble is sufficiently large. Significant secondary nucleation is therefore expected to occur over a limited period in the development of a primary bubble, when both its size and growth rate are sufficiently high. During this time period, theory [38] shows that it is possible for secondary bubble nucleation and growth to occupy a volume as much as two orders of magnitude larger than that occupied by the primary bubble, resulting in flashlike devolatilization in agreement with experiments.

Making the simple assumption for this model that gases are instantaneously transported to bubbles upon generation, then, is a reasonable assumption, especially for polymers such as PMMA that retain long macromolecules during heating and therefore maintain strong elastic properties.

4.2.3 Bubble Migration

Each bubble experiences forces that cause it to move through the melted polymeric material. The internal temperature gradient that results from surface heating of the sphere causes gradients in surface tension and in viscosity, both of which cause the bubble to move toward the heated surface. The bubble is also influenced by the flow fields surrounding neighboring bubbles, including radial fields due to bubble growth as well as convective flow fields. On approach to the surface of the melted thermoplastic sample, deformation of the surface and the bubble occur, and the bubble slows. When bubbles are in close proximity to each other or the sample surface, short range forces such as van der Waals and double-layer forces act to keep bubbles separated while thin-film drainage takes place, resulting in eventual coalescence or surface bursting. The timescale over which coalescence occurs is strongly affected by the presence or absence of surface-acting agents (surfactants) in the melt. Finally, the g-jitter present in a real microgravity environment, such as the NASA Reduced-Gravity Aircraft (± 0.01 g) or the Space Shuttle, results in a randomly-oriented body force proportional to the difference between bubble and melt mass densities.

To simplify this model, flow fields from nearby bubbles and the gravitational force due to g-jitter are neglected. The bubbles are assumed to be far enough apart that each individual bubble can be moved in space as if it is the only bubble in the melt. The only forces that are taken into account, therefore, are those that are caused by viscosity and surface tension gradients, modified by the slowing of velocity as a bubble approaches the surface. The velocity of each bubble, therefore, is in the radial direction only.

The Reynolds number for bubble motion in the polymeric melt, $Re = \rho U(2R)/\mu_p$, is assumed to be much smaller than one, so that the Stokes flow approximation applies. For Stokes flow, the drag force on a bubble of radius R moving in a fluid of infinite extent with terminal velocity U is

$$F_D = 2\pi\mu_p R \left(\frac{2+3\kappa}{1+\kappa} \right) U \quad ,$$
(20)

where the ratio of gas to liquid viscosity is $\kappa = \mu_g/\mu_p \ll 1$ for a bubble in a polymer melt. Multiple forces on a bubble may be linearly superposed. The total bubble velocity is therefore calculated from the summation of individual velocities due to viscosity gradient and surface tension gradient forces.

The viscosity of the molten thermoplastic material depends strongly on temperature and molecular weight, and therefore varies considerably in space and time. The decreasing resistance to movement toward the hot surface of the polymeric sample causes an expanding bubble to move outwards with terminal velocity

$$U_\mu = 2R\dot{R} \left(-\frac{d\ln\mu_p}{dT} \right) \frac{\partial T}{\partial r} \quad ,$$
(21)

where R is the bubble radius, $\dot{R}$ its growth rate, $d\ln_p \mu/dT$ describes the variation of viscosity with temperature (note that the value in parentheses is positive), and $\partial T/\partial z$ is the temperature gradient [17]. This result is based on the assumption that the bubble growth rate is much larger than bubble translation.

The temperature gradient also sets up a non-uniform tangential stress on the surface of a non-contaminated bubble which must be balanced by a flow. This Marangoni, or surface-tension induced, flow is also in the direction of increasing temperature [42]:

$$U_\sigma = \frac{R}{3\mu_p} \left(-\frac{d\ln\sigma}{dT} \right) \frac{\partial T}{\partial r} \quad ,$$
(22)

where $d\ln\sigma/dT$ is the slope of the natural log of surface tension with temperature.

The approach of an axisymmetric deformable particle, either drop or bubble, toward an initially flat interface has been studied by Chi and Leal [43]. The liquids are immiscible, incompressible, and Newtonian. The interface separates the fluid of the dense medium through which the liquid particle moves from the less dense fluid into which the particle will eventually merge. Given the case with like fluids for the particle and outer medium, computations provide a set of curves describing nondimensional velocity as a function of nondimensional distance from the center of mass of the particle to the undeformed flat interface. For a bubble in a polymer melt, the particle-to-fluid viscosity ratio $\lambda = \mu_g/\mu_p$ is low and the capillary number $Ca = \mu_p U_\infty/\omega$, where U_∞ is the particle velocity far from the surface and ω is the surface tension, is high. An empirical fit for the curve most closely representing the case of interest was determined as:

$$f(x) = 0.45879 - 0.070324x + 0.50747\ln(0.5+x) \qquad \text{for } -0.1 < x < 6 \quad ,$$
(23)

where x is the distance between bubble center and undeformed surface nondimensionalized by the radius of the bubble. The velocity of each bubble in the model whose center is closer than six radii from the surface is then decreased through multiplication by this factor. The total radial velocity for a bubble, therefore, is given by

$$ W = f(x) \left[2R\dot{R} \left(-\frac{d\ln\mu_p}{dT} \right) \frac{\partial T}{\partial r} + \frac{R}{3\mu_p} \left(-\frac{d\ln\sigma}{dT} \right) \frac{\partial T}{\partial r} \right] \quad , \tag{24} $$

where $f(x)$ is given by equation (23) for $x = (r_S - r_B)/R_B)$ between -0.1 and 6, by one for $x > 6$, and by zero for $x < -0.1$.

Also of interest from the paper by Chi and Leal [43] is the calculated shape of the film between particle and interface as the particle comes very close to the surface. For bubbles with low λ and high Ca, the film is thinnest directly above the center. This is a geometry that results in rapid bursting of the bubble, as compared to the "dimpled" mode in which the rim is thinnest in a circle some distance from the center.

4.2.4 Bubble Bursting

A critical factor determining the effects of bubbles on the thermal and mass transport behavior of burning thermoplastic materials is the behavior of the bubbles upon reaching the sample surface. If the bubble bursts immediately, the effects are limited to internal transport by the individual bubble. A significant delay in bursting not only slows the delivery of volatile gases to the flame, but could also lead to the development of a foamy insulating surface layer and/or the formation of large bubbles with violent bursting events. Although not addressed by this model, the debris expelled by bursting is of particular interest in microgravity, where gases forceably released by an unattached burning object propel the object in the opposite direction, and where burning droplets may be expelled at high speed.

Upon reaching the surface of a liquid, a bubble may not burst immediately. The deformation of the bubble and the surface interface forms a thin film that must drain and rupture in order for the bubble to release its gases into the surroundings. The physics on the microscopic scale of the liquid membrane is quite different from that controlling the macroscopic bubble motion. At these thicknesses, London-van der Waals and surface tension forces become very important in determining fluid behavior. As was mentioned in the previous subsection, the shape of the thin film is critical to the drainage process. Films whose thinnest point is in the center drain rapidly, while those that are thinnest in a ring near the rim, or "dimpled", are much slower. A dimpled film can develop with time during drainage or be formed at the initial stage. The presence of a surfactant immobilizes the fluid in the film, causing slow drainage regardless of shape.

A theoretical analysis of coalescence time for a draining film between two bubbles in a system without surfactant has been developed by Li and Liu [44]. For a bubble approaching a large planar surface, their expression in CGS measurement units[1] is

$$\frac{1}{t_c} = 25.70 \frac{\sigma^{1.38} B^{0.46}}{\mu_p K^{0.70} F^{0.84} R_B^{1.54}} + 122.17 \frac{\sigma^{1.29} B^{0.26}}{\kappa^{1.02} \mu_p K^{1.70} F^{0.55} R_B^{1.23}} \quad , \tag{25}$$

where σ is the surface tension between the polymer and gas, $\kappa = \mu_g/\mu_p$ is the ratio of viscosities, B is the London-van der Waals constant, and F is the force on the bubble. The parameter K is the curvature of the thin film at the point along the rim at which the pressure within the film equals its local hydrostatic value, calculated as a function of the mobility coefficient M:

$$K = 12.61 + 2.166 \tan^{-1}(2M^{0.8}) \quad , \tag{26}$$

where $M = R_B/(\kappa R_0)$ with R_0 the initial rim radius of the film ($R_B/R_0 \approx 4$).

For immobile films (viscosity ratio $\kappa \to \infty$, resulting in $M \to 0$), the second term in equation (25) is negligible. However, for a bubble in a pure liquid without surfactants, $\kappa \ll 1$, and the second term dominates. The mobility coefficient M is large in this case, and the value of K is about 16. Estimating other parameters as $B \approx 10^{-19}$ erg-cm, $\sigma \approx 50$ dynes/cm, and $\mu_g \approx 2 \times 10^{-4}$ poise, neglecting the first term, and substituting equation (20) for F, the bursting time is approximately

$$t_c \approx 0.3467 \, \mu_p^{0.53} R_B^{1.78} U_B^{0.55} \quad . \tag{27}$$

Large bubbles therefore take longer to burst, as do bubbles travelling with higher velocity. As the melt viscosity decreases with the rising temperature, the bursting time decreases.

Using these expressions, Li and Liu found that coalescence times were on the order of milliseconds for bubbles in a pure liquid in agreement with experiment, as compared to hundreds of seconds for immobile films. Since the effects of thermal degradation of the film are not considered in this coalescence model, however, these timescales are likely to be considerably longer than those actually encountered during bubbling pyrolysis.

The bursting process is accompanied by release of a spray of tiny film droplets around the rim and sometimes by the forceful expulsion of one or more large jet droplets from the rebounding center [22], [23]. In a normal gravity environment, these liquid droplets would fall back into the sample; however, in microgravity the loss of material is permanent. Since these phenomena are not accounted for in this model, the rate of mass loss is expected to be underpredicted.

---

[1]The policy of the National Institute of Standards and Technology is to use SI units of measurement in all its publications. In this document, however, the CGS system of units is sometimes used because of the scales and ranges of the quantities and the wide use of such units in the materials modeling field. For clarification, erg = 10^{-7} J, dyne = 10^{-5} N, and poise = 0.1 N-s/m^2.

4.2.5 Bubble Coalescence

For merging bubbles with radii R_1 and R_2, Li and Liu [44] found the coalescence time for a clean fluid (no surfactants) to be:

$$
\frac{1}{t_c} = 25.70 \frac{\sigma^{1.38} B^{0.46}}{\mu_p K^{0.70} F^{0.84}} \left(\frac{R_1 + R_2}{R_1 R_2} \right)^{1.54} \tag{28}
$$
$$
+ 60.24 \frac{\sigma^{1.29} B^{0.26}}{\kappa^{1.02} \mu_p K^{1.70} F^{0.55}} \left(\frac{R_1 + R_2}{R_1 R_2} \right)^{2.25} (R_1 + R_2)^{1.02} \quad ,
$$

where constants reflect conversion to CGS units. The time for two drops or bubbles of radius R_B to merge is shorter than the time for a single particle of the same radius to burst at an initially flat surface. For a bubble, with small viscosity ratio $\kappa = \mu_g / \mu_p$, the merge time is 0.21 times the bursting time.

This conclusion matches physical intuition, since the shape of the thin film formed by two merging bubbles is more likely to be in the rapid drainage mode with the thinnest spot located in the center.

5 Computational Approach

This computational model of a spherical thermoplastic sample burning in microgravity separates the solution of the energy equation, for which material properties are treated in bulk as purely radial functions, from the calculations of the transport of mass through the polymer melt by means of individual bubbles. This section describes the application of the equations and approaches developed in the Theory section above to the calculations of the evolution of the heated polymeric sphere.

A flowchart outlining the procedure followed at each timestep is presented in Figure 5. The calculations to be described are:

- Mass balance: Given the temperature field, compute the total amount of gas generated in each element.

- Bubble growth: Divide the gas among the bubbles within each element and calculate the new radius and growth rate of each bubble.

- Bubble migration: Use the radius, growth rate, distance from the surface, and local material properties of the polymer melt to determine the velocity of each bubble and locate its final position after this timestep.

- Bubble merging: If bubbles overlap, combine them.

- Bubble bursting: Determine which bubbles have satisfied the requirements for bursting at the sample surface and subtract these gases from the total mass of the sample; determine the resulting mass loss rate.

Bubble Model Flowchart

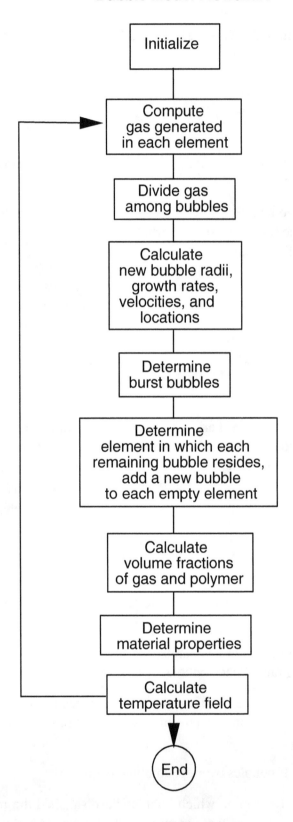

Figure 5: Bubble model flowchart

- Bubble distribution within elements: For bubbles remaining within the sample, determine the elements to which each contributes.

- Bubble nucleation: Nucleate new bubbles, making sure each element contains at least one.

- Bulk material properties: Calculate the volume fractions of gas and polymer within each element and use this information to determine material properties.

- Momentum equations: Consider the swelling due to gasification and shrinkage due to mass (and volume) loss to calculate the radial velocities of gas, polymer, and elements.

- Energy equation: Calculate the radial temperature field at the current timestep from the bulk material properties of each element.

5.1 Geometry

The geometry of the spherical sample is shown in Figure 6. The sample is divided radially into $N - 1$ elements bounded by N nodes forming concentric shells around the center of the sphere. Element thicknesses and node locations change with time, so that the radius of the sample at any time t is given by $r_N = r_S(t)$.

At time $t = 0$, the sample radius is $r_N = r_0$, with a total volume $V_0 = 4\pi r_0^3 / 3$. The sphere is assumed to be homogeneous initially, and each of the $N - 1$ elements is assigned an equal volume,

$$
V_i = \frac{V_0}{(N-1)} = \frac{4\pi r_0^3}{3(N-1)} \quad , \tag{29}
$$

This sets the initial node positions. With node 1 at the center, $r_1 = 0$, node i is initialized at the radial location

$$
r_i = \left(r_{i-1}^3 + \frac{3V_0}{4\pi(N-1)} \right)^{1/3} \tag{30}
$$

for $i = 2, 3, \ldots, N$. Element i is bounded by nodes $i - 1$ and i.

Each element consists of a material volume of polymer plus the gases contained within that region at that timestep. As the polymeric sample gasifies, the nodes defining the element relocate to enclose whatever remains of the polymer originally contained within. For purposes of calculating the bulk material properties of the element, the gas contained by all bubbles within the element is assumed to be evenly distributed throughout the entire spherical shell of the element. For purposes of determining the transport of gases through the sample, however, each bubble k is represented by a sphere of radius R_k located at (r_k, θ_k, ϕ_k), as shown in Figure 7. At the time of "nucleation", the new bubble is assigned a radial location within the element, and its volume is set to zero. The angular coordinates (θ_k, ϕ_k) of the bubble are selected randomly from a distribution for which bubbles are uniformly scattered within the spherical sample volume.

21

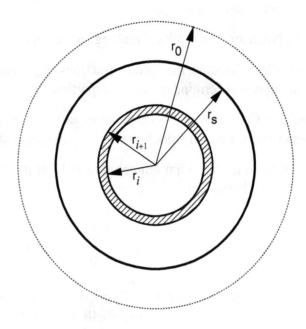

Figure 6: Radial geometry for an element within the spherical sample.

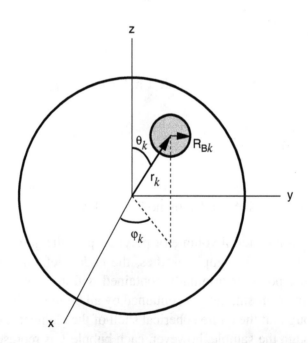

Figure 7: Location of bubble k within the spherical sample.

5.2 Mass Balances

The volume fractions of polymer and gas, ϕ_p and ϕ_g respectively, are taken as uniform within an element. Material properties, such as density, specific heat, and thermal conductivity, are defined at the nodes, and may depend on temperature.

During each timestep, chemical reactions convert some portion of the polymer contained within each element to gas. The mass of this exchanged material is obtained by integrating the rate of change of polymer mass within an element i over the total element volume and multiplying by the time increment $\triangle t$:

$$\triangle M_{pi} = \triangle t \frac{dM_{pi}}{dt} \tag{31}$$

$$= \triangle t \frac{d}{dt} \int_0^{2\pi} \int_0^{\pi} \int_{r_i}^{r_{i+1}} \rho_p \phi_{pi} r^2 \sin\theta \, d\theta \, d\phi \tag{32}$$

$$= -\triangle t \, 4\pi \int_{r_i}^{r_{i+1}} \rho_p \phi_p B e^{-E/RT} r^2 \, dr \quad . \tag{33}$$

This calculation applies the polymer mass balance equation (2) holding the element volume constant (and thus polymer velocity W_p set to zero) over the timestep.

Next, the volume of the polymer that has been lost from element i during this timestep is obtained by dividing the mass by polymer density. Assuming that the polymer density ρ_p is uniform within element i, the rate of loss of polymer volume is

$$\frac{dV_{pi}}{dt} = -4\pi \phi_{pi} B \int_{r_i}^{r_{i+1}} e^{-E/RT} r^2 \, dr \quad , \tag{34}$$

where T is a linear or quadratic function of r from T_i to T_{i+1}, depending on the basis functions chosen for the analysis. The rate of gain of gas volume by element i during this timestep is

$$\frac{dV_{gi}}{dt} = 4\pi \phi_{pi} B \frac{\rho_p}{\rho_g} \int_{r_i}^{r_{i+1}} e^{-E/RT} r^2 \, dr \quad , \tag{35}$$

and the rate of change of total volume of this element is

$$\frac{dV_i}{dt} = \frac{dV_{pi}}{dt} + \frac{dV_{gi}}{dt} = 4\pi \phi_{pi} B \left(\frac{\rho_p}{\rho_g} - 1 \right) \int_{r_i}^{r_{i+1}} e^{-E/RT} r^2 \, dr \quad , \tag{36}$$

5.3 Bubble Growth

To consider the effects of bubbles on the transport of gases to the surface of the sample, the full amount of gas generated in an element during one timestep is considered to instantly diffuse to any bubble extending within the element. This is a simplification that is also consistent with an assumption that secondary nucleation due to elasticity in the melt is significant, as discussed in Section 4.2.2. Bubble dynamics then determine the movement of the gas.

In reality, of course, gases diffuse to a nearby bubble, rather than one that may be located on the opposite side of the spherical shell element. The treatment used here is equivalent to assuming that the rate of gas added to a bubble is determined solely by the temperature at its center, and it neglects the complexity of diffusion from the bubble's nonuniformly heated surroundings. Since more gas will be generated in the hottest region around the bubble, the assumption of a uniformly expanding bubble introduces a bias that slows bubble migration toward the heated surface.

If an element contains more than one bubble, the gases produced during the timestep must be distributed in a reasonable way. For the simple diffusion-controlled bubble growth from equation (18), the growth in bubble volume is linear with radius. An argument can also be made for distributing gases by bubble volume. According to secondary nucleation theory, the rate of change of the mass $\dot{m}_s$ of gas within the secondary bubbles is proportional to the volume of the primary bubble times the nucleation rate I, which increases strongly with radius both in the pre-exponential factor and in the exponent [38]:

$$
\dot{m}_s(t) = \frac{4\pi}{3} \int_0^t I(t-\tau) \frac{R^3(\tau)p_g(\tau)M}{\rho_g R_g T} \, d\tau \quad .
\tag{37}
$$

If secondary nucleation is a dominant factor in this problem, therefore, the gas volume generated in a given element should be distributed among all bubbles within the element in proportion to their volume.

Another approach to distributing gases to bubbles within an element must be taken if the model includes homogeneous nucleation. If bubbles nucleate within an element that already contains bubbles of finite size, distributing gases by bubble size alone eliminates growth for the new bubbles. An alternative distribution method considers any bubble within the element to draw all gas within a zone extending a radial distance ΔR_z from the surface of the bubble. The thickness of this diffusion zone for bubbles within a given element is calculated such that the total volume within all zones contains all of the polymeric melt. Distribution of gases is then made according to the fraction of the polymer volume represented by the diffusion zone around an individual bubble.

Options are also available for distributing gases evenly among bubbles and for distributing by bubble surface area.

5.4 Bubble Migration

The location of each bubble is incremented by its velocity, given in equation (24) as a function of the radius, growth rate, local material properties of the polymer melt, and distance from the sample surface, multiplied by the timestep duration. This calculation is performed in a geometry containing only the polymer melt, to reflect the assumption that bubbles are sufficiently scattered so as not to influence each others' motion. If the bubble is held at the surface to allow for thin-film draining before bursting, it is not allowed to travel further than the position at which its radial velocity is equal to zero.

5.5 Bubble Bursting and Coalescence

Computationally, the phenomenon of bubble bursting is handled by comparing the bubble location and residence time near the surface to the rules that determine its immediate fate. When a bubble breaks the line of the undisturbed surface of the sample, its individual clock is initialized. The bubble is considered to burst when it has remained at the surface for a time period exceeding a specified drainage time, t_d, set to zero for instantaneous bursting. Due to the lack of information on drainage and erosion of a thin polymer film during pyrolysis, the parameter t_d is set to a constant value that allows for a crude investigation of surface effects that may result from the presence of surfactants.

All bubbles that have satisfied the requirements for bursting during the current timestep are removed from the computation. The mass loss rate is then computed by summing the masses of all bubbles that have burst since the end of the previous timestep and dividing by the timestep length:

$$\dot{m} = \sum_{k=1}^{N_b} \frac{\rho_g V_{B\,k}}{\triangle t} \quad . \tag{38}$$

Merging is assumed whenever the volumes of multiple bubbles overlap. The multiple bubbles are replaced by a single bubble whose volume is the sum of the volumes of the merged bubbles and whose center is at their center of mass. This simple approach is supported by the rapid coalescence of two bubbles in a clean fluid as determined by Li and Liu [44] and discussed in subsection 4.2.4. In this case the coalescence time was found to be shorter than the bursting time for a bubble at an initially flat interface by as much as a factor of five.

5.6 Gas Distribution Within Elements

At this point, all of the bubbles that have burst during this timestep have been removed from the sample, and the radial locations and sizes of all of the remaining bubbles are known. The finite element geometry is now reimposed upon the problem in preparation for the determination of bulk material properties for each element.

Given the known quantity of polymer within an element, the task is to determine which bubbles extend into the element and how much of the gas from each of these bubbles lies within the element. As bubbles grow and migrate toward the surface of the spherical sample, many will extend beyond the dimensions of a single element. For the proper determination of the physical properties of these elements, the gases in these bubbles are apportioned by volume over all elements through which they extend. The location of each finite element node is determined as part of this calculation, which progresses from the center of the sample outward.

The basic geometry of a spherical bubble sliced by a sphere delineating the edge of a spherical shell element is shown in Figure 8. Here, the fraction of a small sphere of radius R_b that protrudes above a larger sphere of radius R can be calculated as the difference of sectors of the two spheres cut by a common plane passing through the intersection of the sphere surfaces. The height of the sectors is h_b for the small sphere and h for the larger one. With a representing the distance from the centerline to the surface intersection of the two spheres, and with their centers separated by a distance d, the volume of the small sphere outside of the larger sphere is given by:

$$V = \frac{\pi}{6} \left[h_b(3a^2 + h_b^2) - h(3a^2 + h^2) \right] \quad , \tag{39}$$

where

$$
\begin{aligned}
a^2 &= R_b^2 - (R_b - h_b)^2 \\
h_b &= \frac{(R_b + d)^2 - R^2}{2d} \\
h &= (R - d) - (R_b - h_b)
\end{aligned}
$$

The surface area of this portion of the small sphere is equal to the zone of the sphere sliced by a plane,

$$S = 2\pi R_b h_b \quad . \tag{40}$$

These equations hold for a large sphere slicing through any portion of a small sphere. Setting $d = r_k$, $R_b = R_k$, and $R = r_i$, equation (39) gives the volume of the portion of bubble k contained within element i when the outermost extent of the bubble, $r_k + R_k$, is located within this element. For a bubble k whose innermost point at $r_k - R_k$ is located within element i, the bubble volume contained within the element is equal to the total volume of the bubble minus the portion cut by the sphere defining the outer extent of the element at r_{i+1}:

$$V = \frac{4\pi R_b^3}{3} - \frac{\pi}{6} \left[h_b(3a^2 + h_b^2) - h(3a^2 + h^2) \right] \quad , \tag{41}$$

where again $d = r_k$ and $R_b = R_k$, but in this case $R = r_{i+1}$ in equations for a^2, h_b, and h.

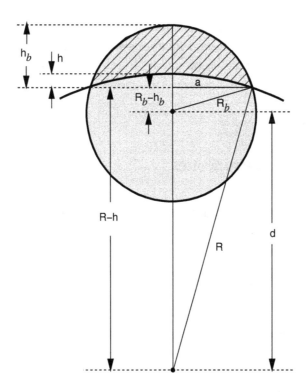

Figure 8: Bubble volume extending beyond a sphere of radius R.

A straightforward but more complex equation can be written for the volume of the midsection of a bubble that extends completely through an element.

Given the radial location of the inner node of an element, the quantity of gas within the element, and therefore the location of the outer node, is determined by iteration. The calculation thus proceeds from the innermost to the outermost element. The gases in portions of unburst bubbles that extend beyond the surface of the sample are assigned to the outermost element.

5.7   Bubble Nucleation

Homogeneous nucleation of new bubbles within an element i of the sample may be explored through use of an Arrhenius expression for the nucleation rate per unit volume,

$$J_i = \phi_{pi} B_N exp(-E_N/RT) \quad , \tag{42}$$

where the pre-exponential factor B_N and activation energy E_N are parameters to be set by the user. The number of nucleation sites to be established within element i during any given timestep is determined by the accumulation of fractional values

$$N_i = N_i + J_i \triangle t \tag{43}$$

for the element over time. Whenever the value of N_i exceeds one, the appropriate number of bubbles of zero volume are distributed at random locations within the element, and the remainder of N_i is left to accumulate toward the next nucleation event. If any element is devoid of bubbles, a nucleation site is provided. At least one bubble is necessary to receive the gases generated within the element during the next timestep.

5.8 Effective Material Properties

Now that the bubble gases have been apportioned among the elements, providing the volume fractions of gas and polymer, $\phi_{gi} = V_{gi}/V_i$ and $\phi_{pi} = V_{pi}/V_i$, for each element i, the bulk material properties of the element can be determined.

The definition of total mass density for element i is

$$\rho_i^* = \rho_{pi}\phi_{pi} + \rho_{gi}\phi_{gi} \tag{44}$$

from equation (5). From the derivation of the energy equation (98) in Appendix A, the equivalent volumetric thermal capacity in element i is

$$(\rho c_p)_i^* = (\rho_p c_{p_p})_i \, \phi_{p_i} + (\rho_g c_{p_g})_i \, \phi_{g_i} \quad . \tag{45}$$

The effective thermal conductivity for each (node/element) is determined from equation (13) as

$$k_i^* = (k_{pi})^{\phi_{pi}} (k_{gi})^{\phi_{gi}} \tag{46}$$

5.9 Component Velocities

The final quantity required to solve the energy equation (7) at the end of this timestep is the barycentric velocity W^*, defined by equation (6). This variable can be determined directly from the total mass conservation equation (4). Similar calculations can be used to determine the individual velocities of polymer and gas components, W_p and W_g.

The finite element approach requires consideration of jump conditions between elements. This arises from the fact that volume fractions are uniform throughout an element and may change considerably from element to element, while material properties such as density and specific heat, often functions of temperature, are continuous across element boundaries.

To determine the barycentric velocity for element i,

$$W_i^* = \frac{\rho_{pi}\phi_{pi}W_{pi} + \rho_{gi}\phi_{gi}W_{gi}}{\rho_i^*} \quad , \tag{47}$$

consider the total mass conservation equation within the element,

$$\frac{\partial \rho_i^*}{\partial t} + \frac{1}{r^2}\frac{\partial}{\partial r}\left(r^2 \rho_i^* W_i^*\right) = 0 \quad . \tag{48}$$

The density ρ_i^*, given by equation (44), is continuous within the element but jumps in value from one element to the next.

Since the node locations r_i and r_{i+1} bounding element i change with time, introduce a linear local coordinate system:

$$x = \frac{2(r - r_i)}{L} - 1 \tag{49}$$

$$r = r_i\left(\frac{1-x}{2}\right) + r_{i+1}\left(\frac{1+x}{2}\right) \quad , \tag{50}$$

where $L_i(t) = (r_{i+1} - r_i)$ is the thickness of the element. This converts nodes at r_i and r_{i+1} to fixed nodes at $x = -1$ and 1 respectively for the element under consideration. Replacing the derivatives with

$$\frac{\partial}{\partial r} = \frac{2}{L_i}\frac{\partial}{\partial x} \tag{51}$$

$$\text{and} \quad \frac{\partial}{\partial t} = \frac{\partial}{\partial t} - \frac{2}{L_i}\left[W_i\frac{(1-x)}{2} + W_{i+1}\frac{(1+x)}{2}\right]\frac{\partial}{\partial x} = \frac{\partial}{\partial t} - \frac{2}{L_i}W\frac{\partial}{\partial x} \quad , \tag{52}$$

where $W_i = dr_i/dt$ and $W_{i+1} = dr_{i+1}/dt$ are velocities of inner and outer nodes respectively, the mass conservation equation can be rewritten as

$$\frac{L_i}{2}r^2\frac{\partial \rho_i^*}{\partial t} + \rho_i^*\frac{\partial}{\partial x}\left(r^2 W\right) + \frac{\partial}{\partial x}\left[r^2 \rho_i^*\left(W_i^* - W\right)\right] = 0 \quad . \tag{53}$$

The nodal velocities are calculated from the node locations at this and the previous timestep as

$$W_i^{k+1} = \frac{\left(r_i^{k+1} - r_i^k\right)}{\Delta t} \quad , \tag{54}$$

where superscripts k and $k+1$ denote successive timesteps. As defined in equation (52), velocity W within the element is interpolated linearly from the nodal velocities.

Integrating this equation within a single element from $x = -1$ to $x = 1$ results in an equation for baryclinic velocity at the outer node given the velocity at the inner node:

$$r_{i+1}^2 \rho_{(i+1)-}^* \left(W_{(i+1)-}^* - W_{i+1} \right) = r_i^2 \rho_{i+}^* \left(W_{(i)+}^* - W_i \right) \tag{55}$$

$$- \frac{L_i}{2} \int_{-1}^1 r(x)^2 \frac{\partial \rho^*}{\partial t} \, dx - \int_{-1}^1 \rho^* \frac{\partial}{\partial x} \left(r^2 W \right) \, dx \quad ,$$

where the subscript $(i+1)-$ indicates a value just within element i from its outer node and $(i)+$ indicates just within from the inner node. For the simplifying case in which polymer and gas densities are considered constant, this equation becomes:

$$r_{i+1}^2 \rho_i^* W_{(i+1)-}^* = r_i^2 \rho_i^* W_{(i)+}^2 - \frac{\partial \rho_i^*}{\partial t} \frac{\left(r_{i+1}^3 - r_i^3 \right)}{3} \quad , \tag{56}$$

with $\rho_i^* = \rho_p \phi_{pi} + \rho_g \phi_{gi}$ uniform throughout the element.

The jump condition in baryclinic velocity from one element to the next is determined by integrating equation (53) carefully from $r_{i+1} - \triangle$ in element i to $r_{i+1} + \triangle$ in element $i + 1$ and taking the limit $\triangle \to 0$. Note that the first two terms in the equation jump in value to the next element without the presence of singularities at the node. The integrated values of these two terms over a narrow region surrounding r_{i+1} therefore goes to zero as the size of the region goes to zero, and the jump condition is

$$\rho_{i+1}^* \left(W_{(i+1)+}^* - W_{i+1} \right) = \rho_i^* \left(W_{(i+1)-}^* - W_{i+1} \right) \quad . \tag{57}$$

The product $\rho^* (W^* - W_i)$ is thus a nodal quantity, although both total density ρ^* and W^* jump from one element to the next. This equation is simply an expression for the conservation of mass flux across element boundaries, in a frame of reference moving with the boundary. It is analogous to the conservation of heat flux across boundaries,

$$\left(k^* \frac{\partial T}{\partial r} \right) \bigg|_{r_{(i+1)+}} = \left(k^* \frac{\partial T}{\partial r} \right) \bigg|_{r_{(i+1)-}} \tag{58}$$

which is automatically enforced by the finite element method, as discussed in Appendix B.

The velocities of the individual components may be determined in a similar way from mass balance equations (2) and (3) for polymer and gas respectively. The resulting equations include a term to account for mass lost or gained. For the simple case in which material properties are assumed constant in time and space, the polymer velocities are given by

$$r_{i+1}^2 \rho_p \phi_{pi} W_{p(i+1)-} = r_i^2 \rho_p \phi_{pi} W_{p(i)+} - \frac{\partial}{\partial t} \left(\rho_p \phi_{pi} \right) \frac{\left(r_{i+1}^3 - r_i^3 \right)}{3} \tag{59}$$

$$-\rho_p \phi_{pi} B \int_{r_i}^{r_{i+1}} r^2 \exp(-E/RT)\, dr$$

$$\text{and} \quad \rho_p \phi_{p(i+1)} \left(W_{p(i+1)+} - W_{i+1} \right) = \rho_p \phi_{pi} \left(W_{p(i+1)-} - W_{i+1} \right) \quad , \tag{60}$$

and gas velocities by

$$r_{i+1}^2 \rho_g \phi_{gi} W_{g(i+1)-} = r_i^2 \rho_g \phi_{gi} W_{g(i)+} - \frac{\partial}{\partial t} (\rho_g \phi_{gi}) \frac{\left(r_{i+1}^3 - r_i^3 \right)}{3} \tag{61}$$

$$+ \rho_p \phi_{pi} B \int_{r_i}^{r_{i+1}} r^2 \exp(-E/RT)\, dr$$

$$\text{and} \quad \rho_g \phi_{g(i+1)} \left(W_{g(i+1)+} - W_{i+1} \right) = \rho_g \phi_{gi} \left(W_{g(i+1)-} - W_{i+1} \right) \quad , \tag{62}$$

Note that even in the frequently investigated limit in which the gas is assumed to escape instantaneously, resulting in volume fractions of $\phi_g = 0$ and $\phi_p = 1$ throughout the sample, the product of $\phi_g W_g$ (given infinite gas velocity) is finite and contributes to the convection of heat in the energy equation.

The consecutive determination of component velocities is begun by fixing the center of the spherical sample, so that $W_{p1} = W_{g1} = W_1^* = 0$.

5.10   Energy Equation

The finite element method [51] was selected for this problem because it easily handles complexities in geometry, including changes in geometry with time and large variations in material properties over space. In this radial model, the sphere is discretized into $N - 1$ spherical shell elements, each of which may change its radial position and volume considerably from timestep to timestep, depending on the radial distribution of bubbles throughout the sphere and on losses from the original polymeric material. Temperatures are determined at every nodal position, and the temperature profile within each element is either linear or quadratic depending on the choice of basis function. Some details of the finite element method for a one-dimensional radial problem are given in Appendix B.

Since the elements are initially equal in volume and the outer elements shrink in size first, the radius of the innermost element is relatively large. Quadratic basis functions were thus used to counter difficulties in meeting the boundary condition at the center of the sphere. Additional nodes at the radial midpoint of each element were added to set up this problem.

Given the polymer volume fraction and bulk values of density, heat capacity, and thermal conductivity for each element, equation (7) is used to determine the temperature at each radial node i at the next time step:

$$\rho c_p^* \left[\frac{\partial T_i}{\partial t} + \frac{(\rho^* W^*)_i}{\rho^*} \frac{\partial T_i}{\partial r} \right] = \frac{1}{r_i^2} \frac{\partial}{\partial r} \left(r_i^2 k^* \frac{\partial T_i}{\partial r} \right) - H_v(\rho_p \phi_p) B \exp^{-E/RT_i} \quad . \tag{63}$$

The initial condition for temperature is uniformly at ambient temperature:

$$T_i(0) = T(r_i, 0) = T_0 \quad . \tag{64}$$

The heat flux boundary condition at the surface of the sphere is

$$-k^* \frac{\partial T}{\partial r} \bigg|_{r_N} = \epsilon q_0 + \epsilon \sigma_{SB} \left(T_N^4 - T_0^4 \right) + h_c(T_N - T_0) \quad . \tag{65}$$

The requirement of a smooth and finite temperature field at the sample center is imposed by

$$\text{at } r_1 = 0, \ \frac{\partial T}{\partial t} = 0 \quad . \tag{66}$$

The finite element formulation results in an easily solved tridiagonal system for linear basis functions and in a nearly block diagonal sparse system for quadratic basis functions. Solution of the quadratic problem is obtained using module DGEABD from the LAPACK scientific computing package.

5.11 Convergence

Every change to the parameters driving this model causes changes to the details of the solution, including number of bubbles at any given timestep, when and where a specific bubble nucleates and how large it grows before it bursts, and so on. Although the details vary considerably, the rate at which the sample loses mass averaged over a time period large compared to a single timestep is relatively stable.

Convergence properties were measured for PMMA with drainage time before bursting of 10 ms. For a fixed number of elements, quadratic convergence was found in time. Convergence was not established in space. However, results fell into a narrow range of values for sufficiently resolved time and space variables. A timestep of 0.25 ms and division of the sample into 40 elements was found to be satisfactory in determining pyrolysis time to better than one percent.

6 Results

The effects of bubble behavior were investigated for two polymers, polymethylmethacrylate (PMMA) and polypropylene (PP), in spheres of diameter 0.3 cm. Input parameters for this model are shown in Table 1. Values were obtained where available from the Polymer Handbook [52]. For this study of bubble effects on a pyrolysis model, material properties are considered constant in time and space, with the exception of polymer viscosity. The variation of polymer viscosity with temperature is determined by the WLF model [53]:

$$\mu_p = \exp\left[13 - \frac{17.44(T - T_{glass})}{51.6 + (T - T_{glass})}\right] \quad . \tag{67}$$

PP	PMMA
$\rho_p = 0.9$ g/cm^3	$\rho_p = 1.17$ g/cm^3
$\rho_g = 0.01$ g/cm^3	$\rho_g = 0.01$ g/cm^3
$(c_p)_p = 2.5$ J/g-K	$(c_p)_p = 1.65$ J/g-K
$(c_p)_g = 2.5$ J/g-K	$(c_p)_g = 1.65$ J/g-K
$k_p = 0.00117$ J/cm-s-K	$k_p = 0.00185$ J/cm-s-K
$k_g = 1.17 \times 10^{-5}$ J/cm-s-K	$k_g = 1.85 \times 10^{-5}$ J/cm-s-K
$\mu_g = 0$ N-s/m^2	$\mu_g = 1.84 \times 10^{-6}$ N-s/m^2
$\sigma = 0.05$ N/m	$\sigma = 0.05$ N/m
$B = 2.4 \times 10^{14}$ s^{-1}	$B = 3.2 \times 10^9$ s^{-1}
$E/R = 26207$ K	$E/R = 17075$ K
$H_v = 800$	$H_v = 1007$
$H_m = 207$	$H_m = 228$
$T_{glass} = 260$ K	$T_{glass} = 378$ K
$\epsilon = 0.92$	$\epsilon = 0.92$
$h_c = 0.001$	$h_c = 0.001$
$MW = 42$ g/mol	$MW = 100$ g/mol

$r_S = 0.15$ cm	
$T_0 = 298$ K	
$q_0 = -6$ W/cm^2	
$t_d = 0$ s	
$\sigma_{SB} = 5.67032 \times 10^{-12}$ W/cm^2-K^4	

Table 1: Nominal parameter values for polypropylene (PP) and polymethylmethacrylate (PMMA).

6.1 PMMA Base Case: Instantaneous Escape of Gases

To illustrate the effects of bubbles on heat and mass transport, comparison will be made to a simple base case in which all gases are assumed to escape from the thermally degrading sample instantly upon gasification. The local volume fractions of polymer and gas under this assumption are constant over time and space with values $\phi_p = 1$ and $\phi_g = 0$ respectively. A potential singularity arises from the instantaneous transport of gas to the surface, making gas radial velocity W_g infinite. This difficulty is resolved by the observation from the mass balance equations (2) and (3) that the product $\phi_g W_g$ is finite. For polymer and gas densities ρ_p and ρ_g constant, this product is

$$\phi_g W_g = -\frac{\rho_p}{\rho_g} W_p = \frac{\rho_p}{\rho_g} \int_0^r r^2 B \exp(-E/RT) dr \quad . \tag{68}$$

In this case, therefore, the barycentric velocity W from equation (6) becomes

$$W = (\rho_p W_p + \rho_g(\phi_g W_g))/\rho_p = 0 \quad , \tag{69}$$

and the energy equation (7) becomes

$$\rho_p (c_p)_p \frac{\partial T}{\partial t} = \frac{1}{r^2} \frac{\partial}{\partial r} \left(r^2 k \frac{\partial T}{\partial r} \right) - H_v \rho_p B e^{-E/RT} \quad . \tag{70}$$

This energy equation may appear to neglect the transport of heat due to the inward movement of the molten polymeric material to fill in the space left by the escaping gas, as has been argued by Staggs [28] for a rectangular geometry. As the analysis makes clear, however, the inward transport of heat energy by the polymer melt is balanced by the outward transport of heat by the escaping gases. Although gases escape instantaneously in this simple model, heat transport due to gas convection cannot be neglected in the equation of energy conservation.

The radius of a spherical PMMA sample exposed to a uniform external heat flux of 60 W/cm^2 is shown as a function of time in Figure 9, with the corresponding mass loss rate vs. time in Figure 10. Initially upon exposure to heat, the sample undergoes preheating. During this time, roughly the first eight seconds in this case, the sample radius remains at the initial value and the mass loss rate is zero. Heat conduction raises internal temperatures, as shown in Figure 11, until they are high enough to cause decomposition of the polymer. The temperature profile within the sample at two second intervals is plotted in Figure 12.

By about ten seconds, as indicated by the knee in the plot of center temperature vs. time in Figure 11, the entire sphere is hot enough to undergo gasification, and the pyrolysis process enters an extended period during which radius decreases linearly with time, surface temperature is nearly steady, and center temperature rises at a slower rate than that during preheating. During this time, the heat energy entering the spherical sample is divided between gasification and conduction.

34

During the final few seconds of pyrolysis, the temperature becomes uniform throughout, and the energy entering the spherical sample is expended in raising its temperature as well as in gasifying the small amount of polymer remaining.

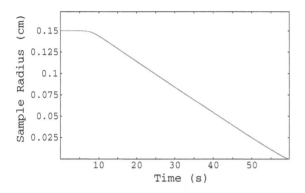

Figure 9: Sample radius vs. time for a spherical PMMA sample exposed to an external heat flux of 60 W/cm^2, assuming instantaneous escape of gases during degradation.

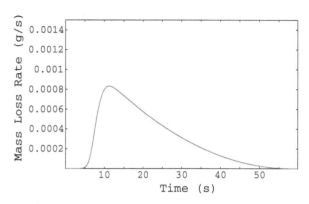

Figure 10: Mass loss rate vs. time corresponding to Figure 9.

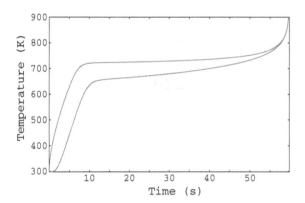

Figure 11: Temperature vs. time at the center (lower line) and on the outer surface of the spherical sample.

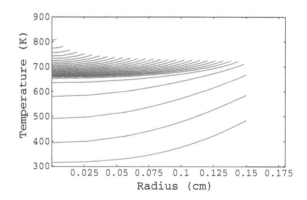

Figure 12: Temperature vs. radius from time $t = 0$ (straight line at $T = 298$ K) to completion of pyrolysis at intervals of 2 s.

6.2 Bubble Generation

With the addition of bubbles to this model, the gases from polymer degradation are no longer expelled instantly upon generation. Instead, these gases add to the volume of "nearby" bubbles, which obey specified rules of migration, coalescence, and bursting.

In a first look at bubble effects, a set of bubble nucleation sites with zero initial volume is placed randomly within the sample, with an initial density of one per finite element. Gases generated within each element are distributed to bubbles contained within or overlapping the element according to the volume of the diffusion region for each as described in section 5.3. New bubbles are nucleated within an element only when it is empty of any other bubbles. When bubbles touch each other, they instantly coalesce, forming a single bubble located at the center of mass of the original bubbles. Decreasing bubble velocity upon approach to the outer surface of the sample is neglected. Bubbles burst as soon as they touch the outer surface, adding their gases to the mass lost during the current time step and disappearing from further calculations.

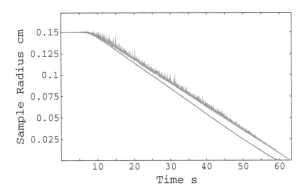

Figure 13: Sample radius vs. time for a spherical PMMA sample exposed to an external heat flux of 60 W/cm^2 with bubbles (orange) and without bubbles (red).

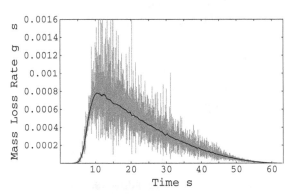

Figure 14: Mass loss rate vs. time corresponding to Figure 13. Black line denotes mass loss rate averaged over 0.5 s.

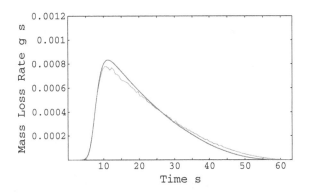

Figure 15: Average mass loss rate vs. time comparing cases with (orange) and without (red) bubbles.

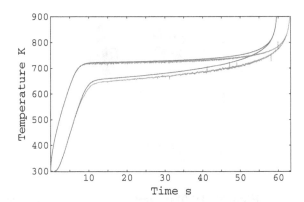

Figure 16: Temperature vs. time at the sample center (lower lines) and on the outer surface for cases with (orange) and without (red) bubbles.

Figure 13 shows the radius as a function of time for a spherical sample divided into 41 finite elements (thus initially containing 41 bubbles). Results for the base case without bubbles, as described in the previous section, are included for comparison. The sample swells with the growth of internal bubbles and contracts when bubbles burst, causing considerable fluctuation in the plot on a fine time scale. These fluctuations are amplified in the plot of instantaneous mass loss rate vs. time in Figure 14. To compare plots of mass loss rate under various conditions, a time average over a period of time long with respect to the rapid fluctuations but short with respect to long-term variations may be used, as shown in the same figure.

A comparison of the time-averaged plot of mass loss rate with mass loss rate when gases escape instantaneously, shown in Figure 15, illustrates that the presence of bubbles slows the pyrolysis process and

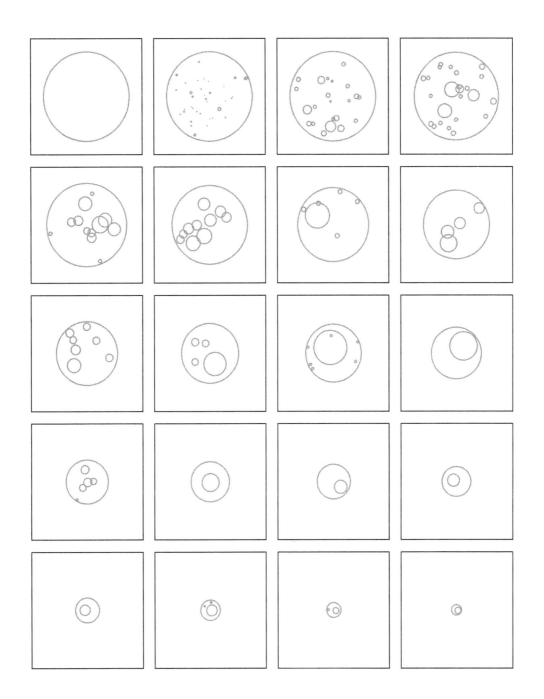

Figure 17: Two-dimensional view of PMMA sample containing bubbles at 3 s intervals beginning at time $t = 0$.

Figure 18: Two-dimensional view of PMMA sample containing bubbles at 0.02 s intervals beginning at time $t = 18$ s.

decreases the average mass loss rate. This is due to the insulating effects of the retained gases, whose thermal conductivity is considerably less than that of the polymeric melt. The effect is demonstrated in Figure 16, which shows that the temperature at the center of the sample is lower throughout pyrolysis for the case including bubbles than for the case without.

A view of bubbles within the spherical sample at various times during pyrolysis is given in Figure 17. During preheating and early gasification all bubbles are small; in later stages of pyrolysis some bubbles may become quite large in comparison to the size of the sample before they burst. Over the much shorter time period covered by the sequence in Figure 18, individual bubbles may be observed as they grow to the bursting point. Migration may also be observed in this sequence, though the axis of migration for a particular bubble is not likely to be aligned with the selected view.

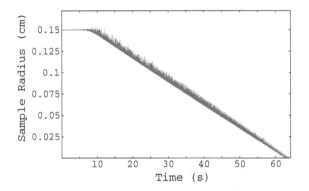

Figure 19: Sample radius vs. time for PMMA showing a lack of sensitivity to gas distribution.

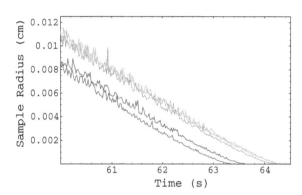

Figure 20: Same as Figure 19 magnified at the end of pyrolysis. In order of increasing final times, gases are distributed to bubbles evenly, by bubble radius, by diffusion zone volume, by surface area, and by bubble volume.

If an element contains a portion of more than one bubble, the gases generated within that element during the next time step must be distributed among these bubbles. The model allows for distribution linearly by bubble radius, by bubble surface area, or by bubble volume. Gases may alternatively be distributed evenly among bubbles or by diffusion zones of the same thickness for all bubble portions within the element. Figures 19 and 20 show that the results are insensitive to how gas is distributed among bubbles, at least for this set of model assumptions. This is likely to be due in part to the low number of bubbles populating the sample during most of the pyrolysis process.

6.3 Bursting Effects

To study the potential effects of bubble bursting dynamics on pyrolysis of the spherical polymeric sample, bubbles are assigned individual drainage clocks. As each bubble approaches the surface, its velocity is slowed according to the factor discussed in section 4.2.3. When the bubble breaks the plane of the surface, drainage is assumed to begin, and the clock is started. When the clock exceeds the predetermined drainage time, which is provided as an input parameter to the problem, the bubble bursts and releases its gases.

Figures 21 and 22 show that a delay in bubble bursting on the order of tens of milliseconds has a considerable effect on the pyrolysis rate for the PMMA sphere. The plot of radius as a function of time shows that the additional retention of gases in bubbles causes swelling of the sphere after the initial preheating period. When the bubbles that gather at the surface early in the process finally burst, they release a large amount of gas at once, as seen in the spikes for time-averaged mass loss rate around time t=8 s for drainage times of 20 ms and 30 ms. After this event, a decrease in mass loss rate sets in due to the thermal insulation of the interior of the sample by the increased amount of gas at the surface.

The number of finite elements used for these runs was 41, with timesteps of duration 0.25 ms.

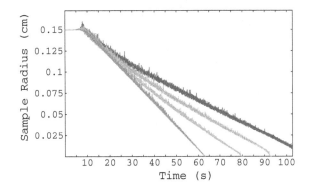

Figure 21: Sample radius vs. time for bubbling PMMA sphere with bursting occurring a time period $t_d = 0$ ms (orange), 10 ms (yellow), 20 ms (green), and 30 ms (blue) after a bubble touches the sample surface.

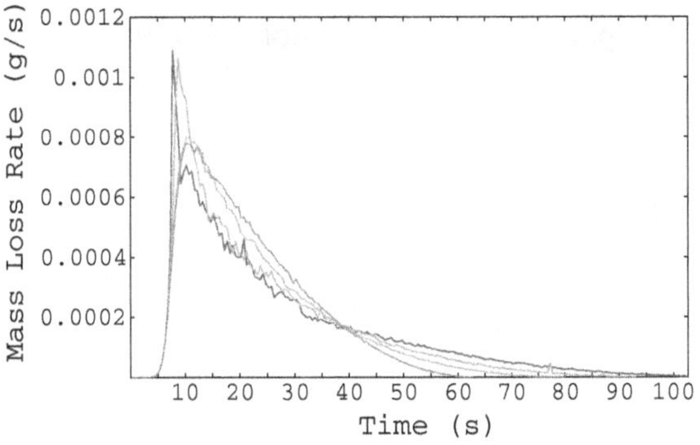

Figure 22: Mass loss rate vs. time corresponding to Figure 21. Mass loss rates are averaged over 0.5 s.

Thermal effects of the bubbles with time are demonstrated in Figures 23 through 25. Large fluctuations in the temperature of the outer surface with time reflect the formation and bursting of the bubbles. The size of the temperature fluctuations increases as drainage time, and therefore the amount of gas close to the surface, increases. In each of these plots the temperatures at the outer surface and the center of the spherical sample are compared to those for a sample whose bubbles burst instantly (zero drainage time). The thermal insulation effects of the bubbles undergoing drainage before bursting are apparent in the lowered temperatures at the surface after bubbles have burst (the minimum temperatures for the upper plots) and at the sample center.

The effects of surface bubbles on the temperature profile within the spherical sample are shown more clearly in Figures 26 and 27, with profiles of temperature vs. radius plotted every 2 s. When each bubble bursts as soon as it reaches the surface, the thermal conductivity of the outermost element does not change significantly from that of the polymeric melt. However, when each bubble is held at the surface before bursting, as in Figure 27, the thermal conductivity of the outermost element may be much smaller than the melt, resulting in a large jump in temperature over a small distance near the surface.

Figure 28 presents a sequence of views of the PMMA sample with thin-film drainage times of 20 ms. Note that many of the bubbles are clearly located along the sample surface preparing to burst.

40

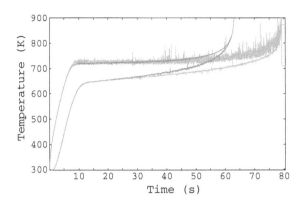

Figure 23: Temperature vs. time at the sample center (lower lines) and on the outer surface for drainage times $t_d = 10$ ms (yellow) and 0 ms (orange).

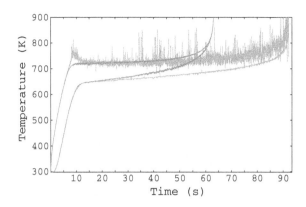

Figure 24: Temperature vs. time at the sample center and outer surface for drainage times $t_d = 20$ ms (green) and 0 ms (orange).

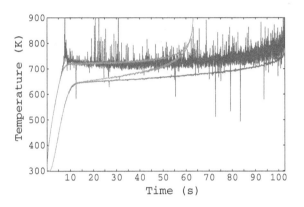

Figure 25: Temperature vs. time at the sample center and outer surface for drainage times $t_d = 30$ ms (blue) and 0 ms (orange).

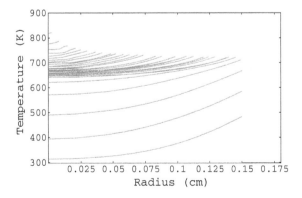

Figure 26: Temperature vs. radius at intervals of 2 s for bursting time $t_d = 0$ s.

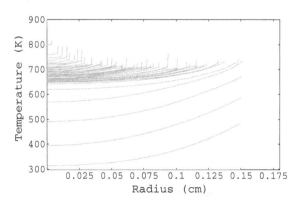

Figure 27: Temperature vs. radius at intervals of 2 s for bursting time $t_d = 20$ ms.

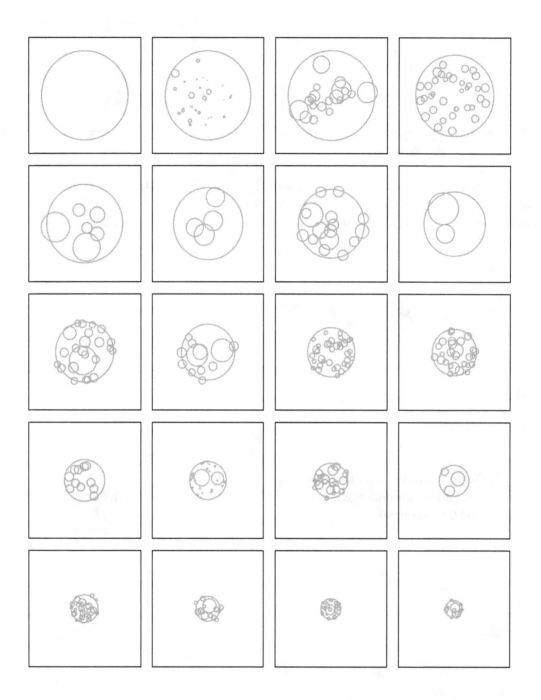

Figure 28: Two-dimensional view of bubbling PMMA sample with drainage time of 20 ms. Frames are shown at 4 s intervals beginning at time $t = 0$.

6.4 Nucleation Effects

As discussed in section 5.7, the rate of bubble nucleation per unit volume is assumed to take the form of the Arrhenius expression

$$J = \phi_p B_N \exp\left[-E_N/RT\right] \quad . \tag{71}$$

The pre-exponential factor B_N determines the magnitude of the nucleation rate, while the activation energy E_N determines how rapidly the rate increases with temperature. To study what effect nucleation rate has on the behavior of a sample undergoing pyrolysis, pre-exponential factor B_N is varied while activation energy E_N is held at a fixed value. With a temperature of 730 K at the surface during the quasi-steady period of pyrolysis in the absence of bubbles (see Figure 16), the value of E_N is arbitrarily set such that the nucleation rate at 600 K drops to roughly 10 % of the rate at the surface. This study fixes the thin-film drainage time before bubbles are allowed to burst at 20 ms.

Surprisingly, the nucleation rate has little effect on the rate at which the polymeric sphere pyrolyzes, as shown in Figure 29. The 20 ms drainage case from the previous chapter, for which nucleation was limited to ensuring at least one bubble per element, is included for comparison, plotted in green as previously. The increase in sample radius, or swelling, is slightly larger for the highest nucleation rate, and the time of peak swelling corresponds to that of the maximum number of bubbles shown in Figure 30. Although early in the pyrolysis process the total number of bubbles present in the sample at a given time reflects the nucleation rate, by 40 s the number drops to values fluctuating between zero and the number of elements, the same range traversed in the absence of the Arrhenius nucleation model.

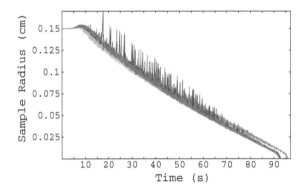

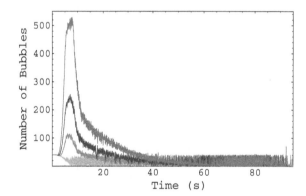

Figure 29: Sample radius vs. time for bubbling PMMA sphere with nucleation defined by $B_N = 1 \times 10^{11}$ (s-cm^3)$^{-1}$ (light blue), 2×10^{11} (s-cm^3)$^{-1}$ (navy), and 4×10^{11} (s-cm^3)$^{-1}$ (purple) with $E_N/R = 7500$ K. Case without an Arrhenius nucleation model is shown in green. Drainage time for bursting bubbles is 20 ms.

Figure 30: Number of bubbles in sample vs. time corresponding to Figure 29.

Figure 31 shows a time sequence from 0 s to 76 s for bubble nucleation obeying an Arrhenius expression with $B_N = 2 \times 10^{11}$ (s-cm^3)$^{-1}$. At $t = 8$ s (the third frame), when the number of bubbles is at its

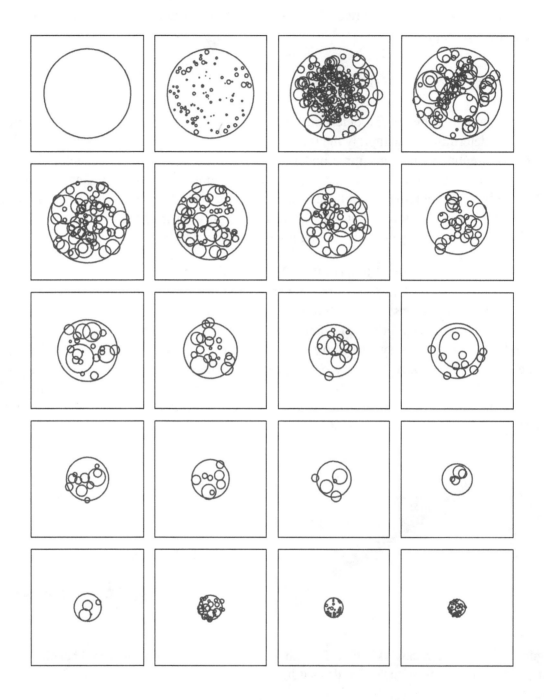

Figure 31: Two-dimensional view of bubbling PMMA sample with Arrhenius-based nucleation scheme with $B_N = 2 \times 10^{11}$ (s-cm^3)$^{-1}$ and $E_N/R = 7500$ K. Drainage time is 20 ms and time interval between frames is 4 s.

peak of about 250, the bulk of the bubbles is well within the sample, with relatively few bubbles located at the surface and preparing to burst. Although the nucleation scheme requires the density of nucleation sites to increase with temperature and therefore with radial location within the sample, bubbles near the surface quickly travel through the melt of low viscosity to the surface and burst after 20 ms. According to the model, then, bubbles do not accumulate at the surface. This does not agree with experimental observations of combustion in microgravity in which a layer of growing, relatively monodisperse bubbles covers the surface of the spherical sample during the first few seconds of combustion. The fixed value of drainage time in the model clearly underestimates the time before bursting during this early period.

6.5 Bubbles in Polypropylene (PP)

To look at the effects of including bubbles in the pyrolysis calculations for polypropylene, the same two cases are considered as for PMMA in sections 6.1 and 6.2. For the base case, all gases generated during a timestep immediately escape the sample. For the simplest case including bubbles, the problem is initialized with one nucleation site per element and new bubbles are added only to empty elements. The bubbles burst as soon as they contact the surface of the spherical sample. The number of elements in the sphere is 41 for these runs, and the timestep is 0.25 ms.

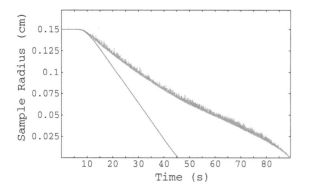

Figure 32: Sample radius vs. time for a spherical PP sample exposed to an external heat flux of 60 W/cm^2 with bubbles (orange) and without bubbles (red).

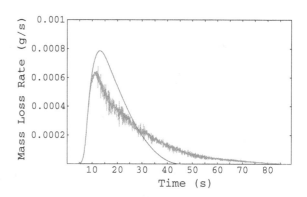

Figure 33: Mass loss rate vs. time corresponding to Figure 32.

The effects for bubbles in PP are considerably larger than for PMMA. Figures 32 and 33 show that the presence of bubbles causes mass loss rate to drop considerably after 10 s and doubles the pyrolysis time. Compare this to the roughly 10 % increase in pyrolysis time for bubbling PMMA under identical assumptions, as shown in Figure 13. The thermally insulating effect of the bubbles related to this drop in mass loss rate is shown in Figure 34. Although the outer surface of the sample heats to the same temperature as the case without bubbles, the center of the sample remains cooler after the initial pre-heating. An extended quasi-steady period of slow interior heating follows.

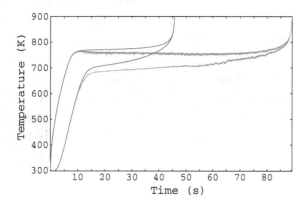

Figure 34: Temperature vs. time at the sample center (lower plots) and outer surface (upper plots) corresponding to Figure 32.

7 Conclusions

This model verifies that the presence of bubbles has a considerable impact on heat and mass transfer. The results illustrate areas where further research is most needed to provide an accurate depiction of the effects of bubbling within burning thermoplastic materials.

Pyrolysis is found to be particularly sensitive to the bursting process. Because of the insulating effects of bubbles that retain a significant amount of gas within the sample, increasing the delay time before bursting by tens of milliseconds causes a significant decrease in mass loss rate. To accurately predict these effects, a much better physical model of the bursting process is needed. The improved model should include both degradation and drainage of the polymeric thin film in the heated environment. In addition, the bursting process results in a fine droplet spray as the thin film ruptures, with the potential to expel a center droplet as the liquid surface rebounds. In microgravity, these events will carry polymeric melt away from the sample, thus increasing the effective mass loss rate. Experiments and computational models that improve our understanding of these phenomena are needed to determine their effects on microgravity combustion of thermoplastic materials.

An improved model of bursting behavior will naturally provide a better physical description of bubble merging, and vice versa. Although it was not used in this model, a spring constant to maintain distance between bubbles has been applied successfully to studies of foam flow [55] and could be used in similar models to keep bubbles separate during the thin-film drainage process.

As polymers burn, gaseous degradation products are generated in-depth. Some gaseous molecules are created at sufficiently close proximity to form bubble nucleation sites, some are distributed among existing bubbles, and others remain in solution in the melt. Gases may not be generated uniformly within the heated material, as demonstrated by recent research on secondary nucleation in which rapid gasification was discovered in regions of high elastic strain surrounding growing bubbles. More work to understand the dynamic behavior of gases at the molecular level is necessary to be able to predict bubble behavior with a greater degree of confidence.

Nucleation, bubble merging, and gas partitioning among bubbles did not appear to have strong effects on the pyrolysis process in the results from this model. However, these phenomena are critical in determining the number and size distribution of bubbles. Their influence may be much more apparent if it is determined, for example, that time to bursting is strongly dependent on radius.

References

[1] Kimzey, J.H., et al., "Flammability in Zero-Gravity Environment," NASA TR R-246, 1966.

[2] "Flammability, Odor, and Offgassing Requirements and Test Procedures For Materials In Environments That Support Combustion." NASA NHB 80.60.1B, NASA TM-84066, 1981.

[3] Kashiwagi, T. and Ohlemiller, T.J., "A Study of Oxygen Effects on Nonflaming Transient Gasification of PMMA and PE During Thermal Irradiation," 19th Symposium (International) on Combustion, The Combustion Institute, 1982.

[4] Olson, S.L. and Sotos, R.G., "Combustion of Velcro in Low Gravity," NASA TM 88970, 1987.

[5] Greenberg, P.S., Sacksteder, K.R., and Kashiwagi, T., "The USML-1 Wire Insulation Flammability Glovebox Experiment," *Third International Microgravity Combustion Workshop*, NASA Lewis Research Center, Cleveland, Ohio, April 11-13, 1995.

[6] Yang, J.C. and Hamins, A., "Combustion of a Polymer (PMMA) Sphere in Microgravity," *Third International Microgravity Combustion Workshop*, NASA Lewis Research Center, Cleveland, Ohio, April 11-13, 1995.

[7] Yang, J.C., Hamins, A., and Donnelly, M.K., "Combustion of a Polymer (PMMA) Sphere in Microgravity," NISTIR 6331, 1999.

[8] Wichman, I.S., "A Model Describing the Steady-State Gasification of Bubble-Forming Thermoplastics in Response to an Incident Heat Flux," *Comb. and Flame* 63:217–229 (1986).

[9] Cagliostro, D.E. , Riccitiello, S.R., Clark, K.J. and Shimizu, A.B., "Intumescent Coating Modeling," *J. Fire & Flamm.* 6:205–220 (1975).

[10] Anderson, C.E. and Wauters, D.K., "A Thermodynamic Heat Transfer Model for Intumescent Systems," *Int. J. Engrg. Sci.* 22:881–889 (1984).

[11] Buckmaster, J., Anderson, C. and Nachman, A., "A Model for Intumescent Paints," *Int. J. Engng. Sci.* 24:263–276 (1986).

[12] Anderson Jr., C.E., Ketchum, D.E., and Mountain, W.P., "Thermal Conductivity of Intumescent Chars," *J. Fire Sci.* 6:390–410 (1988).

[13] Attar, A., "Bubble Nucleation in Viscous Material Due to Gas Formation by a Chemical Reaction: Application to Coal Pyrolysis," *AIChE J.* 24:106–115 (1978).

[14] Oh, M.S., "Softening Coal Pyrolysis," Doctoral thesis, M.I.T. Dept. of Chem. Eng. (1985).

[15] Oh, M.S., Peters, W.A., and Howard, J.B., "An Experimental and Modeling Study of Softening Coal Pyrolysis," *AIChE J.* 35:775–792 (1989).

[16] Schiller, D., Bhatia, R., and Sirignano, W.A., "Energetic Fuel Droplet Gasification With Liquid-Phase Reaction," Conference Proceedings, 15th International Colloquium on the Dynamics of Explosions and Reactive Systems, July 31–August 4, 1995, pp. 438-441.

[17] Butler, K.M., Baum, H.R., and Kashiwagi, T., "Three-Dimensional Modeling of Intumescent Behavior in Fires," *Proceedings of the Fifth International Symposium*, International Association on Fire Safety Science, pp. 523–534 (1997).

[18] Butler, K.M., "Bursting Bubbles from Combustion of Thermoplastic Materials in Microgravity," *Proceedings from Fifth International Microgravity Combustion Workshop*, NASA/CP–1999-208917, NASA Glenn Research Center, Cleveland, Ohio, pp. 93–96 (1999).

[19] Chan, W.R.,Kelbon, M. and Krieger, B.B., "Modelling and Experimental Verification of Physical and Chemical Processes During Pyrolysis of a Large Biomass Particle," *Fuel* 64:1505–1513 (1985).

[20] Roberts, W.L. and Driscoll, J.F., "A Laminar Vortex Interacting with a Premixed Flame: Measured Formation of Pockets of Reactants," *Comb. and Flame* 87:245–256 (1991).

[21] Renard, P.-H., Thevenin, D., Rolon, J.C., Candel, S., "Dynamics of Flame/Vortex Interactions," *Prog. Energy & Comb. Sci.* 26:225–282 (2000).

[22] Newitt, D.M., Dombrowski, N., and Knelman, F.H., "Liquid Entrainment 1. The Mechanism of Drop Formation from Gas or Vapour Bubbles," *Trans. Instn. Chem. Engrs.* 32:244–261 (1954).

[23] Tomaides, M. and Whitby, K.T., "Generation of Aerosols by Bursting of Single Bubbles," in Liu, B.Y.H., ed., *Fine Particles; Aerosol Generation, Measurement, Sampling, and Analysis*, Academic Press, Inc., New York, pp. 235–252 (1976).

[24] Madorsky, S.L., *Thermal Degradation of Organic Polymers*, John Wiley & Sons, Inc., New York (1964).

[25] Lengelle, G., "Thermal Degradation Kinetics and Surface Pyrolysis of Vinyl Polymers," *AIAA J.* 8:1989–1996 (1970).

[26] Kansa, E.J., Perlee, H.E., Chaiken, R.F., "Mathematical Model of Wood Pyrolysis Including Internal Forced Convection," *Comb. & Flame* 29:311–324 (1977).

[27] DiBlasi, C., "Analysis of Convection and Secondary Reaction Effects Within Porous Solid Fuels Undergoing Pyrolysis," *Comb. Sci. & Tech.* 90:315–340 (1993).

[28] Staggs, J.E.J., "A Theoretical Investigation into Modelling Thermal Degradation of Solids Incorporating Finite-Rate Kinetics," *Comb. Sci & Tech.* 123:261–285 (1997).

[29] Staggs, J.E.J., "A Simple Model of Polymer Pyrolysis Including Transport of Volatiles," *Fire Safety J.* 34:69–80 (2000).

[30] Kaviany, M., *Principles of Heat Transfer in Porous Media*, Springer-Verlag, New York (1991).

[31] Shafi, M.A. and Flumerfelt, R.W., "Initial Bubble Growth in Polymer Foam Processes," *Chem. Eng. Sci.* 52:627–633 (1997).

[32] Kwak, H-Y and Kim, Y.W., "Homogeneous Nucleation and Macroscopic Growth of Gas Bubble in Organic Solutions," *Int. J. Heat Mass Transfer* 41:757–767 (1998).

[33] Blander, M. and Katz, J.L., "Bubble Nucleation in Liquids," *AIChE J.* 21:833–848 (1975).

[34] Han, J.H. and Han, C.D., "Bubble Nucleation in Polymeric Liquids. II. Theoretical Considerations," *J. Poly. Sci. B* 28:743–761 (1990).

[35] Han, J.H. and Han, C.D., "Bubble Nucleation in Polymeric Liquids. I. Bubble Nucleation in Concentrated Polymer Solutions," *J. Poly. Sci. B* 28:711–741 (1990).

[36] Vrentas, J.S. and Duda, J.L., "Molecular Diffusion in Polymer Solutions," *AIChE J.* 25:1–24 (1979).

[37] Gent, A.N. and Tompkins, D.A., "Nucleation and Growth of Gas Bubbles in Elastomers," *J. Appl. Phys.* 40:2520–2525 (1969).

[38] Yarin, A.L., Lastochkin, D., Talmon, Y., and Tadmor, Z., "Bubble Nucleation During Devolatilization of Polymer Melts," *AIChE J.* 45:2590–2605 (1999).

[39] Olson, S.L., "Buoyant Low Stretch Stagnation Point Diffusion Flames Over a Solid Fuel," Doctoral thesis for Dept. of Mech. and Aero. Eng. at Case Western U. (1997).

[40] Epstein, P.S. and M.S. Plesset, "On the Stability of Gas Bubbles in Liquid-Gas Solutions," *J. Chem. Phys.* 18:1505–1509 (1950).

[41] Venerus, D.C., Yala, N., Bernstein, B., "Analysis of Diffusion-Induced Bubble Growth in Viscoelastic Liquids," *J. Non-Newt. Fluid Mech.* 75:55-75 (1998).

[42] Young, N.O., Goldstein, J.S. and Block, M.J., "The Motion of Bubbles in a Vertical Temperature Gradient," *J. Fluid Mech.* 6:350–356 (1959).

[43] Chi, B.K. and Leal, L.G., "A Theoretical Study of the Motion of a Viscous Drop Toward a Fluid Interface at Low Reynolds Number," *J. Fluid Mech.* 201:123–146 (1989).

[44] Li, D. and Liu, S., "Coalescence between Small Bubbles or Drops in Pure Liquids," *Langmuir* 12:5216–5220 (1996).

[45] Chen, S., Wang, Z., Shan, X., and Doolen, G.D., "Lattice Boltzmann Computational Fluid Dynamics in Three Dimensions," *J. Stat. Phys.* 68:379–400 (1992).

[46] Personal communication from X. Shan, Los Alamos National Laboratory, August 1995.

[47] Williams, F.A., *Combustion Theory*, The Benjamin/Cummings Publishing Company, Inc., Menlo Park (1985).

[48] Law, C.K., "Recent Advances in Droplet Vaporization and Combustion," *Prog. Energy Combust. Sci* 8:171–201 (1982).

[49] Chang, K.-C. and Shieh, J.-S., "Theoretical Investigation of Transient Droplet Combustion by Considering Flame Radiation," *Int. J. Heat Mass Transfer* 38:2611–2621 (1995).

[50] Woods, L.C., *The Thermodynamics of Fluid Systems*, Oxford University Press, New York, NY (1975).

[51] Reddy, J.N. and D.K. Gartling, *The Finite Element Method in Heat Transfer and Fluid Dynamics*, CRC Press, Inc., Boca Raton, FL (1994).

[52] Brandrup, J. and Immergut, E.H., eds., *Polymer Handbook, 3rd ed.*, Wiley-Interscience, New York, NY (1989).

[53] Brydson, J.A, *Flow Properties of Polymer Melts, 2nd ed.*, George Godwin Ltd, London, England (1981).

[54] Carslaw, H.S. and Jaeger, J.C., *Conduction of Heat in Solids*, Clarendon Press, Oxford (1959).

[55] Durian, D.J., "Foam Mechanics at the Bubble Scale," *Phys. Rev. Let.* 75:4780–4787 (1995).

A   Appendix A - Temperature Equation Derivation

An equation for temperature in a multicomponent fluid can be derived directly from the principles of irreversible thermodynamics [50]. Assume thermodynamic equilibrium among all components k (such as gas and polymeric melt in this paper), so that $T_k = T$. A fundamental relation of thermodynamics states that

$$du = T\,ds - p\,d\left(\frac{1}{\rho}\right) + \sum_k g_k\,dc_k \quad , \tag{72}$$

where u is the specific internal energy (energy / mass), s the specific entropy, p pressure, ρ density, g_k the chemical potential (also known as the specific Gibbs free energy) for component k, and $c_k = \rho_k \phi_k / \rho$ is the mass concentration of component k. Note that the mass per total volume, often represented in the thermodynamic literature as ρ_k, is given here by $\rho_k \phi_k$ with ρ_k the material density of the component, in accordance with the notation used in this document. For this multicomponent fluid, the total density is the sum of the densities of individual components, pressure is the sum of the partial pressures, and the total specific internal energy and entropy are the sums of individual values weighted by the mass concentration of each value:

$$
\begin{aligned}
\rho &= \sum \rho_k \phi_k \quad ; & p &= \sum p_k \quad ; \\
u &= \sum c_k u_k \quad ; & s &= \sum c_k s_k \quad .
\end{aligned}
\tag{73}
$$

The internal energy may also be written as a function of the alternate set of variables $u(T, \rho, c_k)$. The exact differential form for $s(T, \rho, c_k)$ is

$$ds = \left(\frac{\partial s}{\partial T}\right)_{\rho,c_k} dT + \left(\frac{\partial s}{\partial \rho}\right)_{T,c_k} d\rho + \sum \left(\frac{\partial s}{\partial c_k}\right)_{T,\rho,c_{(k)}} dc_k \quad , \tag{74}$$

where the subscript notation $c_{(k)}$ indicates that all mass concentrations c_m are held constant except for $m = k$. Replacing ds in equation (72) results in

$$du = T\left(\frac{\partial s}{\partial T}\right)_{\rho,c_k} dT + \left[T\left(\frac{\partial s}{\partial \rho}\right)_{T,c_k} + \frac{p}{\rho^2}\right] d\rho + \sum \left[T\left(\frac{\partial s}{\partial c_k}\right)_{T,\rho,c_{(k)}} + g_k\right] dc_k \quad . \tag{75}$$

All three partial derivatives in s can be written in terms of physical quantities. The first relates directly to the specific heat at constant specific volume, defined as

$$c_v = T\left(\frac{\partial s}{\partial T}\right)_\rho \quad . \tag{76}$$

The other two may be written in terms of the expansivity β and isothermal compressibility κ_T,

$$\beta = -\frac{1}{\rho}\left(\frac{\partial \rho}{\partial T}\right)_p \qquad\qquad \kappa_T = \frac{1}{\rho}\left(\frac{\partial \rho}{\partial p}\right)_T \qquad\qquad (77)$$

whose quotient is

$$\frac{\beta}{\kappa_T} = \left(\frac{\partial p}{\partial T}\right)_\rho \qquad . \qquad\qquad (78)$$

From any exact differential $dS = X\,dx + Y\,dy$, the Maxwell relations

$$\left(\frac{\partial X}{\partial y}\right)_x = \left(\frac{\partial Y}{\partial x}\right)_y \qquad\qquad (79)$$

may be obtained. Using the fundamental relation for the specific Helmholtz free energy,

$$df = -s\,dT + \frac{p}{\rho^2}\,d\rho + \sum_k g_k\,dc_k \qquad , \qquad\qquad (80)$$

the relations

$$\left(\frac{\partial s}{\partial \rho}\right)_T = -\frac{1}{\rho^2}\left(\frac{\partial p}{\partial T}\right)_\rho = -\frac{\beta}{\rho^2 \kappa_T} \qquad\qquad (81)$$

and $\quad \left(\frac{\partial s}{\partial c_k}\right)_{T,c_{(k)}} = -\left(\frac{\partial g_k}{\partial T}\right)_{c_k} \qquad\qquad (82)$

are derived.

Substituting for the partial derivatives of s in equation (75) results in

$$du = c_v\,dT + \left[\frac{p}{\rho^2} - \frac{\beta T}{\rho^2 \kappa_T}\right]d\rho + \sum \left[g_k - T\left(\frac{\partial g_k}{\partial T}\right)_{\rho,c_{(k)}}\right]dc_k \qquad . \qquad\qquad (83)$$

Finally, replacing exact differentials with full time derivatives, $d/dt = \partial/\partial t + \mathbf{v}\cdot\nabla$, multiplying by ρ, and rearranging terms, an equation for temperature can be written as

$$\rho c_v \frac{dT}{dt} = \rho\frac{du}{dt} - \frac{1}{\rho}\left[p - \frac{\beta T}{\kappa_T}\right]\frac{d\rho}{dt} - \sum\left[g_k - T\left(\frac{\partial g_k}{\partial T}\right)_{\rho,c_{(k)}}\right]\rho\frac{dc_k}{dt} \qquad . \qquad\qquad (84)$$

At this point, the physics of the problem is applied to determine the terms on the right hand side. The mass balance of each component requires

$$\rho \frac{dc_k}{dt} = -\nabla \mathbf{J}_k + \overset{+}{\rho}_k \quad , \tag{85}$$

where

$$\mathbf{J}_k = \rho_k \phi_k \mathbf{w}_k = \rho_k \phi_k (\mathbf{v}_k - \mathbf{v}) \tag{86}$$

is the diffusion momentum for component k, $\mathbf{v} = \sum (\rho_k \phi_k \mathbf{v}_k)/\rho$ is the barycentric velocity, and $\overset{+}{\rho}_k$ is the rate of change of mass per volume for component k due to chemical reactions. Total mass conservation gives

$$\frac{d\rho}{dt} = -\rho \nabla \cdot \mathbf{v} \quad . \tag{87}$$

The internal energy balance for a multicomponent fluid is given by

$$\rho \frac{du}{dt} = -\nabla \cdot \mathbf{q} + \boldsymbol{\sigma} : \nabla \mathbf{v} - \sum_k \mathbf{J} \cdot \left[\frac{\nabla \cdot (-p_k \mathbf{I} + \boldsymbol{\pi}_k)}{\rho_k} \right] \tag{88}$$
$$- \sum_k \frac{|\mathbf{v}_k|^2}{2} (\nabla \cdot \mathbf{J}_k) + \Psi + \sum \sum a_{kj} \frac{|\mathbf{v}_k - \mathbf{v}_j|^2}{2} \quad ,$$

where $\mathbf{q}$ is the heat flux vector

$$\mathbf{q} = \sum \left[\mathbf{q}_k - \boldsymbol{\pi} : \nabla \mathbf{v} + \mathbf{J}_k \left(u_k + \frac{p}{\rho} + \frac{|\mathbf{w}_k|^2}{2} \right) \right] \quad , \tag{89}$$

$\boldsymbol{\sigma}$ is the stress tensor

$$\boldsymbol{\sigma} = p\mathbf{I} + \boldsymbol{\pi} = \sum p_k \mathbf{I} + \sum \boldsymbol{\pi}_k \quad , \tag{90}$$

with $\boldsymbol{\pi}$ the viscous stress tensor, Ψ is heat added due to radiation, and a_{kj} is the rate per unit volume at which component k gains mass from component j due to chemical reactions.

Applying these conservation equations to equation (84) results in the temperature equation

$$\rho c_v \frac{dT}{dt} = -\nabla \cdot \mathbf{q}^* - \frac{\beta T}{\kappa_T} \nabla \cdot \mathbf{v} + \Psi + \boldsymbol{\pi} : \nabla \mathbf{v} + \sum T \mathbf{J}_k \cdot \mathbf{X}_k^J - \sum \left(g_k + \frac{|\mathbf{v}_k|^2}{2} \right) \overset{+}{\rho}_k \tag{91}$$
$$+ \sum T \left(\frac{\partial g_k}{\partial T} \right)_{c_k} \left[-\nabla \cdot \mathbf{J}_k + \overset{+}{\rho}_k \right] + \sum \sum a_{kj} \frac{|\mathbf{v}_k - \mathbf{v}_j|^2}{2} \quad ,$$

55

where

$$\mathbf{q}^* = \mathbf{q} + \mathbf{J}_k \left(\frac{|\mathbf{v}_k|^2}{2} - g_k \right) \tag{92}$$

and

$$\mathbf{X}_k^J = -\frac{1}{T} \left[\frac{\nabla \cdot (-p_k \mathbf{I} + \boldsymbol{\pi}_k)}{\rho_k} + \nabla \left(\frac{|\mathbf{v}_k|^2}{2} - g_k \right) \right] \quad . \tag{93}$$

The constitutive relations are derived in the usual way from requiring the local specific entropy to increase with time, and the final temperature equation is

$$\rho c_v \left(\frac{\partial T}{\partial t} + \mathbf{v} \cdot \nabla T \right) = \nabla \cdot (k^* \nabla T) - \frac{\beta T}{\kappa_T} \nabla \cdot \mathbf{v} + \Psi + \Phi - \sum g_k \overset{+}{\rho}_k \tag{94}$$

$$+ T \sum \left(\frac{\partial g_k}{\partial T} \right)_{c_k} \left[-\nabla \cdot \mathbf{J}_k + \overset{+}{\rho}_k \right] + \sum \sum a_{kj} \frac{|\mathbf{v}_k - \mathbf{v}_j|^2}{2} \quad ,$$

where k^* is the thermal conductivity of the multicomponent fluid. The first term on the right hand side is heat transported by conductivity, and the second term is heat generated by changes in pressure. The third term describes heat transported by radiation. The fourth is the positive definite sum of all terms describing heat loss due to energy dissipation,

$$\Phi = \mu \nabla \mathbf{v} : \nabla \mathbf{v} + \frac{\mu}{3} (\nabla \cdot \mathbf{v})^2 + \sum D_k |\mathbf{v}_k - \mathbf{v}|^2 \quad , \tag{95}$$

with μ as the absolute viscosity of the fluid and D_k as a set of positive coefficients that describes heat generated due to diffusion of one species into another. The fifth term is heat generated by chemical reactions, and the sixth accounts for the dependence of chemical potentials on temperature. The seventh term describes the heat flux due to the kinetic energy generated when one component chemically changes into another. This term penalizes large differences in velocity between components, preventing, for example, the instantaneous removal of gas from the sample.

The relation between the specific heat at constant volume for the multicomponent fluid and the material properties of the individual components can be determined by formulating this same problem by summing the individual internal energies, giving

$$c_v = \frac{\sum (\rho_k \phi_k c_{v_k})}{\sum (\rho_k \phi_k)} \quad . \tag{96}$$

The thermal conductivity of the fluid is modelled as some physically reasonable combination of the properties of individual components.

Note that the specific heat at constant volume c_v appears in the temperature equation rather than the specific heat at constant pressure c_p. The expression

$$c_p - c_v = \frac{\beta^2 T}{\rho \kappa_T} \tag{97}$$

relates these two quantities.

To simplify the problem, several assumptions are made. All heat losses due to radiation are assumed to occur at the surface of the sphere, eliminating the internal radiation term, Ψ. The variation of chemical potential with temperature is assumed small. Energy dissipation Φ is neglected. Finally, both polymer and gas are assumed incompressible, eliminating the terms containing expansivity β and $\nabla \cdot \mathbf{v}$. Using these assumptions and replacing $\overset{+}{\rho}_k$ with the Arrhenius expression, the energy equation for this spherically symmetric geometry is

$$(\rho c_p)\left[\frac{\partial T}{\partial t} + W\frac{\partial T}{\partial r}\right] = \frac{1}{r^2}\frac{\partial}{\partial r}\left(r^2 k^* \frac{\partial T}{\partial r}\right) - \left[H_v - \frac{|W_g - W_p|^2}{2}\right]\rho_p\phi_p B\exp^{-E/RT} \tag{98}$$

where $H_v = g_g - g_p$ is the (positive) heat of vaporization and W_p and W_g are the radial velocities of polymer and gas respectively.

Note that this formulation of the equation for temperature for a multicomponent fluid varies from that applied to the thermal degradation of wood by Kansa et al. [26] and DiBlasi [27] and to polymers by Staggs [28], [29]. These models neglect kinetic and potential energy and replace internal energy with enthalpy and specific enthalpy with $h = c_p(T - T_0)$. As has been shown here, these assumptions are unnecessary.

B Appendix B - The Finite Element Method

The goal of the finite element method [51] is to determine an approximate solution T^e that satisfies the differential equation and its boundary conditions through the means of a variational or weighted-integral method. The method is illustrated here for a linear set of basis functions.

To begin, the radial energy equation (7) is written in weak Galerkin form:

$$\int_0^{r_S} h(r) \left\{ \rho c_p \left(\frac{\partial T^e}{\partial t} + W \frac{\partial T^e}{\partial r} \right) + H_v \dot{m}^e - \frac{1}{r^2} \frac{\partial}{\partial r} \left(kr^2 \frac{\partial T^e}{\partial r} \right) \right\} r^2 dr = 0 \quad . \tag{99}$$

The approximate solution T^e that is sought is one for which a weight function $h(r)$ can be found that satisfies the equation over the entire domain in a weighted-integral sense. An integration by parts on the term that contains the highest order derivative results in the equation

$$\int_0^{r_S} h(r) \left[\rho c_p \left(\frac{\partial T^e}{\partial t} + W \frac{\partial T^e}{\partial r} \right) + H_v \dot{m}^e \right] r^2 dr \tag{100}$$

$$+ \int_0^{r_S} kr^2 \frac{\partial h}{\partial r} \frac{\partial T^e}{\partial r} dr - kr^2 h(r) \frac{\partial T^e}{\partial r} \Big|_0^{r_S} = 0 \quad .$$

Note that this integration by parts has reduced (weakened) the polynomial order required of the solution T^e by shifting some of the differentiation to the weight function. The temperature solution is now required to be only linearly continuous throughout the domain; that is, the first derivative of temperature may now be discontinuous.

(The integration described above is actually performed over the entire spherical domain. Since neither the weight function $h(r)$ nor the quantity in curly brackets depends on angle θ or ϕ, integration has been performed over both angles, and the resulting factor of 4π has been divided out.)

The domain of the problem is now subdivided into subdomains called finite elements. If a solution can be found that solves the above weighted-integral equation in each individual element without sacrificing the necessary continuity between elements, then the desired approximate solution has been found.

From equation (100), the equation that must hold in each element i bounded by nodes at radii r_i and r_{i+1} is

$$\int_{r_i}^{r_{i+1}} \left\{ h(r) \left[(\rho c_p) \left(\frac{\partial T}{\partial t} + W \frac{\partial T}{\partial r} \right) + H_v \dot{m} \right] + k \frac{\partial h}{\partial r} \frac{\partial T}{\partial r} \right\} r^2 dr \tag{101}$$

$$- \delta_{i(N-1)} kr_S^2 h \frac{\partial T}{\partial r} \Big|_{r_S} = 0 \quad .$$

58

Note that the boundary condition is applied only for the outermost element, for which $i = N - 1$, where N is the number of nodes.

A local coordinate system is now defined,

$$z = \frac{2(r - r_i)}{L} - 1 \quad , \tag{102}$$

with $L(t) = (r_{i+1}(t) - r_i(t))$ the radial thickness of the element. The average radius of element i is defined as $r_{av} = (r_i + r_{i+1})/2$. Since within the element neither the weighting function h nor the temperature solution T requires more than a first order polynomial, these functions can be represented as a sum of nodal values multiplied by a set of linear basis functions,

$$h(z) = \sum_{j=1}^{2} h_j(z) \tag{103}$$

and

$$T(z, t) = \sum_{j=1}^{2} T_j(t) h_j(z) \quad , \tag{104}$$

where $h_1 = (1 - z)/2$ and $h_2 = (1 + z)/2$. The heat sink term can be described similarly as

$$\dot{m}(z, t) = \sum_{j=1}^{2} \dot{m}_j(t) h_j(z) \quad , \tag{105}$$

where $\dot{m}_j = \rho_p \phi_p B \exp(-E/RT_j)$ is the value of the Arrhenius expression at the local node j. This change of coordinates relates the global numbering of nodes i and $i + 1$ bounding element i to local node numbers $j = 1$ and 2 respectively.

Substituting the local coordinate system into equation (101) and applying the outer boundary condition from equation (65) results in the following matrix equation for element i:

$$[B] \frac{\partial}{\partial t} \{T\} + ([C] + [A]) \{T\} + [G] \{\dot{m}\} + \{K\} = 0 \tag{106}$$

where

$$B_{lj} = (\rho c_p) \frac{L}{2} \int_{-1}^{1} h_l h_j \left((r_{av})^2 + z r_{av} L + \frac{L^2 z^2}{4} \right) dz \tag{107}$$

$$C_{lj} = (\rho c_p)W \int_{-1}^{1} h_l \frac{\partial h_j}{\partial z} \left((r_{av})^2 + z r_{av} L + \frac{L^2 z^2}{4} \right) dz \tag{108}$$

$$A_{lj} = k \frac{2}{L} \int_{-1}^{1} \frac{\partial h_l}{\partial z} \frac{\partial h_j}{\partial z} \left((r_{av})^2 + z r_{av} L + \frac{L^2 z^2}{4} \right) dz \tag{109}$$

$$G_{lj} = H_v \rho_p \phi_p B \int_{-1}^{1} h_l h_j \left((r_{av})^2 + z r_{av} L + \frac{L^2 z^2}{4} \right) dz \tag{110}$$

$$\dot{m}_j = \exp(-E/RT_j) \tag{111}$$

$$K_j = 0, \qquad i \neq N-1 \text{ or } j = 1 \tag{112}$$
$$= r_S^2 \epsilon q_0 + \epsilon \sigma \left(T_N^4 - T_0^4 \right) + h_c (T_N - T_0), \qquad i = (N-1) \text{ and } j = 2 \quad.$$

After integration, the matrices become

$$[B] = (\rho c_p) \frac{L}{6} \begin{bmatrix} 2(r_{av})^2 - r_{av}L + L^2/5 & (r_{av})^2 + L^2/20 \\ (r_{av})^2 + L^2/20 & 2(r_{av})^2 + r_{av}L + L^2/5 \end{bmatrix} \tag{113}$$

$$[C] = (\rho c_p) \frac{W}{6} \begin{bmatrix} -[3(r_{av})^2 - r_{av}L + L^2/4] & 3(r_{av})^2 - r_{av}L + L^2/4 \\ -[3(r_{av})^2 + r_{av}L + L^2/4] & 3(r_{av})^2 + r_{av}L + L^2/4 \end{bmatrix} \tag{114}$$

$$[A] = \frac{k}{L} \begin{bmatrix} (r_{av})^2 + L^2/12 & -[(r_{av})^2 + L^2/12] \\ -[(r_{av})^2 + L^2/12] & (r_{av})^2 + L^2/12 \end{bmatrix} \tag{115}$$

$$[G] = H_v \rho_p \phi_p B \frac{L}{6} \begin{bmatrix} 2(r_{av})^2 - r_{av}L + L^2/5 & (r_{av})^2 + L^2/20 \\ (r_{av})^2 + L^2/20 & 2(r_{av})^2 + r_{av}L + L^2/5 \end{bmatrix} \quad. \tag{116}$$

The next step in setting up the finite element problem is assembling the matrices from individual elements to form a single linear algebra equation to be solved. The two requirements for connecting the entire domain are continuity of temperature and balance of heat flux from one element to the next. The first requirement is satisfied by using the global numbering of nodes to sum matrices of individual elements in the correct positions. The final matrices $[B]$, $[C]$, $[A]$, and $[G]$ are $N \times N$ tridiagonal matrices. The second requirement is satisfied automatically by the finite element method as a "natural" boundary condition. To see this, consider again the radial energy equation in weak Galerkin form (99), but this time consider only the portion of the integration carried out over two adjacent elements a and b, with thermal conductivities k_a and k_b. These elements are defined by nodes $a1$ and $a2$ and nodes $b1$ and $b2$ respectively, where nodes $a2$ and $b1$ are identical and shared. Performing an integration by parts on the highest order derivative term in the weak Galerkin equation integrated from node $a1$ to node $b2$ results in an integrated part plus boundary terms:

$$\int_{r_{a1}}^{r_{a2}} \{\ldots\} r^2 dr - k_a r^2 h(r) \frac{\partial T^e}{\partial r} \bigg|_{r_{a1}}^{r_{a2}} + \int_{r_{b1}}^{r_{b2}} \{\ldots\} r^2 dr - k_b r^2 h(r) \frac{\partial T^e}{\partial r} \bigg|_{r_{b1}}^{r_{b2}} = 0 \quad. \tag{117}$$

The integrated parts have been set to 0 through the formulation of the linear algebra equation as already described. Since the boundary terms must also sum to zero, it must be true that at shared nodes the terms must be equal. At node $a2/b1$ therefore,

$$-k_a \frac{\partial T^e}{\partial r}\bigg|_{r_{a2}} + k_b \frac{\partial T^e}{\partial r}\bigg|_{r_{b1}} = 0 \quad . \tag{118}$$

This is precisely the required condition that heat flux is matched from one element to the next.

In the final step to prepare the finite element problem to be solved, the differentiation in time is considered. From equation (106), the equation for the entire domain is

$$[B]\frac{\partial \{T\}}{\partial t} + ([C] + [A])\{T\} + [G]\{\dot{m}\} + \{K\} = 0 \quad , \tag{119}$$

where the matrices have been assembled from those for individual elements. This equation is treated numerically by using the standard tools for partial differential equations to set up the matrix equation

$$[\mathcal{A}]\{T^{n+1}\} = [\mathcal{B}]\{T^n\} - \{\mathcal{C}\} \tag{120}$$

to determine the nodal temperatures at the next timestep $t_{n+1} = t_n + \triangle t$ from the temperatures at the current timestep t_n. For the Crank-Nicolson scheme used in the code for this model, the matrices in this equation are

$$\mathcal{A} = \left[\frac{2}{\triangle t}\frac{([B^n] + [B^{n+1}])}{2} - ([C^{n+1}] + [A^{n+1}]) \right] \tag{121}$$

$$\mathcal{B} = \left[\frac{2}{\triangle t}\frac{([B^n] + [B^{n+1}])}{2} + ([C^n] + [A^n]) \right] \tag{122}$$

$$\mathcal{C} = 2\left([G^{n+1}]\{\dot{m}^{n+1}\} + \{K^{n+1}\}\right) \quad . \tag{123}$$

The superscripts n and $n + 1$ for vectors $\{T\}$, $\{\dot{m}\}$, and $\{K\}$ refer to the application of values of temperature at the previous timestep and those to be determined at this timestep, respectively. Note that $\{\dot{m}^{n+1}\}$ and $\{K^{n+1}\}$ appear in the RHS of this equation The values in these vectors are determined iteratively at each timestep until the solution converges. The superscripts n and $n + 1$ for the matrices $[A]$, $[B]$, $[C]$, and $[G]$ indicate that element sizes and material properties from previous and current timesteps respectively are applied.

Since all matrices in this equation are tridiagonal, the solution for each timestep is obtained quickly and easily. The finite element code written for this model was verified by comparison with an analytical solution for heat transport in a sphere [54].

For quadratic basis functions, h_1 and h_2 are replaced by the set

$$
\begin{aligned}
h_1 &= -\frac{z}{2}(1-z) \\
h_2 &= (1-z^2) \\
h_3 &= \frac{z}{2}(1+z) \quad,
\end{aligned}
\tag{124}
$$

and the solution is obtained using a sparse matrix solver.

www.ingramcontent.com/pod-product-compliance
Lightning Source LLC
Chambersburg PA
CBHW080603060326
40689CB00021B/4921